In *Confessions of an Abusive Hu...*
covered abuser, offers a 12-step recovery program for those prone
to abusive behavior.

—*Publishers Weekly*

Your book, *Confessions of an Abusive Husband,* is superb! The
tone is positive, challenging and accountable. The content is com-
prehensive and well organized. I'm looking forward to completion
so we can integrate it into our program.

As a counselor working in this field and as a director of a large
treatment program, I thank you for the sweat, the tears, the joy,
and the love that went into *Confessions.* This book will be a very
significant resource for men in recovery.

—*Glenn Rose, M.A., L.M.F.T.,*
Men's Resource Center

In *Confessions of an Abusive Husband,* Robert Robertson takes
a courageous look at the dark underbelly of his former penchant
toward domestic violence and emerges into the light with unprec-
edented hope and help for any person with an anger or violence
problem.

—*Tamera Smith Allred,*
This Week Magazine

As I deliberate on how to begin this review of Robertson's book, I wonder as to how many ways I can say Bravo- Splendid- Commendable- Good job. If I were seated in front of the author I would applaud him.

You see, Mr. Robertson has accomplished a difficult but needed task. He's supplied the reading public with this much needed book on an emotionally charged subject. The subject is wife abuse.

Confessions of an Abusive Husband is ... a clear, painfully honest look at the abusive husband and the total effect that it has on all parties involved in the situation. The book studies this abuse thoroughly and honestly, giving an understanding of the cycle and the means in which to break the cycle.

Having myself been on the receiving end of an abusive relationship, I have to say that Robert Robertson pulls no punches describing the terrible effect that emotional abuse can have on the very strongest of people.

Confessions of an Abusive Husband is a great asset to both male and female. Having a balanced, healthy relationship with win-win situations is necessary for a wholeness of any partnership. This book would also be a great learning experience for young people who have been a part of an abusive family situation. I am pleased to have had the privilege of reading this book. There is much value between its covers. Bravo Mr. Robertson.

—*Carletta Mayer*
Friend's Review

"...And as I hung up the phone, it occurred to me: he'd grown up just like me. My boy was just like me."

"Cats in the Cradle"
Courtesy of Story Songs Ltd
Copyright 1974

This book is my attempt to break the chain of abusive behavior that is passed on from generation to generation. The story centers on my own recovery and my involvement with other men in recovery. The stories and examples of abuse are real, and, unfortunately, similar stories occur in many families on a regular basis. It doesn't have to continue—the solution is now available.

This book is dedicated to Emotionally Repressed Men (ERMs), my Brothers in Anger, everywhere. My greatest desire is that we may heal together.

Robert Robertson, 1992

Confessions of an

ABUSIVE HUSBAND

A How-To Book for "Abuse-Free" Living for Everyone

By Robert Robertson, M.A.

Robertson, Robert.
    Confessions of an abusive husband : a how-to book for
abuse-free living / Robert Robertson.
    p. cm.
    ISBN 0-9631739-0-1

    1. Wife abuse—Psychological apsects. 2. Abusive men—
Psychological aspects. I. Title.

HV6626.H6 1992   362.8292
                    QBI91-2018

        Typesetting and cover refinement by
            Post Haste Publishing, Inc.

Inquiries, orders, and catalog requests should be addressed to

        Heritage Park Publishing Company
                P. O. Box 126
            Lake Oswego, OR 97034

Published in the United States
10 9 8 7 6 5 4 3 2 1

ACKNOWLEDGMENTS

To list all of the influences in my recovery, and their contribution to this book would be impossible; however, I feel a special thanks is necessary to the following:

First, my Heavenly Family for guiding me down the path of recovery and easing the burdens.

Second, to the authors of all of the books I used to aid in my recovery and whose ideas sometimes I share in my book—(a) Daniel Sonkin, PhD. and Michael Durphy, M.D., for *Learning to Live Without Violence*, the book that brought me out of denial and made me examine my behavior; (b) John Bradshaw, for *Homecoming*, which taught me to grieve for my inner child and champion him; (c) David D.Burns, M.D., for *Feeling Good, The New Mood Therapy*, for clearing up my cognitive disorders; (d) Drs. Jordan and Margaret Paul, for *Do I Have To Give Up Me to Be Loved By You*, for getting me on the path to learn; (e) Matthew McKay, PhD., Peter Rogers, PhD., and Judith McKay, R.N., for *When Anger Hurts*, for further quieting the storm within me; and (f) M. Scott Peck, M.D., for *The Road Less Traveled*, for showing me the difficulties of life and how to overcome them with grace.

Third, Men's Resource Center Counseling (especially Joe Mitchell) for my first group counseling; my men's anger groups for their support in mutual healing; and Ranae Johnson and Rundi for their assistance.

Fourth, my former wife, Kate, for making me face hard choices.

Fifth, my current friends for their love, support, and advice.

Sixth, Berdell Moffett for consulting;Richard Kent Matthews (who went the extra mile) for editing; Bob Cain and Hazel Billings for readership comments; Peggy Newell, PhD., for professional comments; and Pam Stevers for cover design. Their help was invaluable in completing this project.

Seventh, and finally, my typist and friend, Jeri, for her continual support, encouragement, and listening ear.

Without all of the above, this book would not have been possible.

TABLE OF CONTENTS

Robert Robertson

Confessions of an Abusive Husband

INTRODUCTION

My Story Of Abuse

The first time I was abusive to my wife was on the eve of our wedding. She had neglected to renew the insurance on her car. In the event of an automobile accident, I knew I would be liable as soon as we were married. Because of her negligence, I yelled at her and called her names. I concluded by saying, "If you or I were in a wreck, no matter who is at fault, I would have to pay. Even bankruptcy won't eliminate a lawsuit. I would be tied down financially my whole life!" This established a pattern of abuse that was to become my way of "teaching" her to behave in an appropriate manner (according to Bob).

Five years later, the abuse had escalated to more than emotional battering. I needed more force to "teach" her now. I came home one evening after work to find the house a mess. Instead of cleaning, my wife, Kate, had spent the day canning peaches. "This place needs to be cleaned up. I can't live in a mess like this. You need to get organized." To reinforce my point, I grabbed a metal shelf on which approximately 60 jars of peaches were neatly stored and pulled it over. They crashed to the floor and splattered all over the utility room. Glass fragments, peaches, and juice were everywhere. "Get Organized!" I yelled, as I stormed out of the house.

Six years after the peach incident, the abuse had escalated further. Kate and I were seeing our fourth marriage counselor. He stated, "Bob, you'd better learn to control your anger." So I did — I stuffed my feelings away so deeply that the next time I blew up I dragged her down the stairs by her hair and threatened to kill her! This was the last straw for Kate — we separated shortly thereafter and were divorced.

Not only was I abusive at home, I considered myself an "equal opportunity abuser" — at work with employees and customers, while driving, on the telephone, or any time I had a conflict with another person. Being abusive was my way of handling all my problems. When I owned my own contracting business, I would blow up at my employees or customers whenever I felt angry or pressured in any way. Twice, when driving, I had motioned to other drivers to pull off the road to talk and ended up swinging my fist through their window to hit them! Once, when someone confronted me on the phone, I left in a hurry to go looking for him. Fortunately, he was nowhere to be found.

I was a rage-aholic! I was out of control. I was frightened by my behavior and would shake uncontrollably for hours after each incident. For days I would be filled with shame and guilt and regret. Yet my abusive episodes would happen again and again with regular consistency. I am lucky my behavior never got me arrested during my marriage. But it did cost me my wife and family, and a great deal of physical and emotional pain.

Why was I abusive? Why couldn't I control my anger? Why did I behave this way? Surely I knew better, right?

After our final separation, I reflected on my life to determine why I had been abusive in my marriage. It was not for lack of setting goals. Eighteen years ago, at the age of twenty-five, and three years before my marriage, I was unhappy with my situation. I was uneducated, financially unstable, practicing poor health habits, and failing in all my social relationships. I set goals in several areas of my life and was determined to make permanent changes in my behavior and circumstances.

The first area I decided to improve was my education. Three times before I had started college only to drop out without finishing a semester. This time I started and completed both a Bachelors and Masters program. At the same time I set new physical goals. I stopped smoking and drinking, and began to work out with weights. I gained over twenty pounds of lean weight and felt great. Yet I was acting out in an angry and abusive manner.

After completing college and starting a family, I looked at my financial condition. I decided to start my own contracting business. Within a few years my business was doubling annually and I received an award for outstanding contractor in my field. Realizing the importance of getting along socially, I improved my public speaking skills and became more friendly and outgoing. Yet I was still acting out in an angry and abusive manner.

My emotional goal was to increase love for myself and others. Finally, I worked on spiritual goals, serving my church in teaching and leadership positions. My life centered on my family, church, and career. I projected an image to my associates of the ideal, successful family man. Yet I continued acting out in an angry and abusive manner.

Why?

I really didn't want to behave this way. In fact, all of the men I know who are abusive are deeply ashamed of their behavior. In the past I would simply stuff away my anger, thinking, "Everything is OK, all is under control." I felt that as long as I kept a lid on my emotions, everything would be all right. But sooner or later I would always explode. The cycle continued unabated through twelve years of marriage and became more frequent and intensified as time passed. I was frustrated and out of control.

Not only was I abusive, I denied responsibility for my actions, claiming my wife "made" me angry. I minimized my actions, insisting that I had merely pushed her away instead of striking her. I continued this behavior — denial, abuse, remorse and determination to stop — over and over until it was too late, until I lost my wife and children.

Again I asked, "Why?"

Now, three years after our final separation, I know why. The answer to this question is now available and I've interwoven it into my story. The rage I felt within, the angry voices in my head, have been quieted. The feelings of loneliness and isolation have been filled. The abusive behavior has stopped and the stress of my life lessened. I now allow myself to feel the primary feelings of grief and shame and choose to explore the secondary feeling of anger and its underlying causes. I choose to solve problems assertively and not abusively. The hole within my soul is filled with peace and calmness. This was not a magical event but a long process; however, the price was well worth the result.

Why This Book?

I've tried several times to begin this book, but always stopped. I saw a real need for such a book, but felt ashamed to be its author. Now, I feel it is necessary to do so for the following reasons:

One: There are lots of myths and misconceptions involved in anger and abusive behavior. Both abusers and abused will be surprised at some of the answers they find here. These answers come not only from my research but also from my own recovery and involvement with other men in recovery.

Two: I want to assist others who want to change their abusive behavior. I feel the best way to do this is to help abusers to become aware that there is a problem and that there are treatment options. Most abusers fail to recognize that they even have a problem, or they minimize it to the point where it doesn't seem to exist. The power of denial is strong in abusers. I will explain later why that is so. *The first and essential step in recovery is recognizing that there is a problem. The second step is to take responsibility for correcting that problem.*

Three: I consider this book to be a personal catharsis, a labor of love. As I examine my own life, I feel there must have been a reason or purpose for what happened to me. Looking back over the barren landscape of my life through the eyes of recovery, I feel like the Phoenix rising out the ashes; I, too, must reassemble my life and rise above my situation. Writing this book has released me from the grief of the past and marks the beginning of a marvelous new life. I'm doing that by living in the *now* and enjoying each moment to the fullest.

About This Book

I have written this book in three parts. Part One defines the problem and gives definitions for the what, when, where, and why of abusive behavior. In Part Two, I talk about the treatment of abusive behavior, which should always take place with an empathetic and qualified counselor. The treatment, outlined in twelve steps, begins with stopping the violence and then progressively continues to eliminating its source. Part Three shows the contexts of abusive behavior, with family relationships and the work place being emphasized. Finally, in the Appendix, I have shown how to monitor abusive behavior through anger journals.

Also, this book is "written by the numbers," with many of the behavior changes listed as first, second, etc. As Patrick Carnes pointed out in his book, *Don't Call It Love*, (1991), Adult Children (those who grew up in dysfunctional families) need things spelled out, in logical steps, in order to make changes in their lives and to learn the appropriate behavior.

This book is dedicated to all those who are involved in an abusive relationship. If you so allow, this book will help you recognize your problem and show you how to change your behavior. I first want to say, however, that a lot of work is required — a lot of work, a lot of tears, and a lot of pain.

I conduct men's anger groups and workshops on abusive behavior. Some men call me and say they want to join the group but then change their minds and don't show up. More come for the first meeting and then drop out. Many more will come to several meetings and then drop out, claiming that they are "cured." I liken this to the cure of an infection with a single shot of penicillin: generally the problem persists. It takes time — at least two years. It took years for us to become abusive, and it takes years to overcome being that way. There are no shortcuts; I've looked painstakingly and found none.

Mostly this is a book of hope, a source of help. You now have a hammer (your anger) and all of your problems resemble nails. I hope to put into your toolbox several tools which will help you solve life's problems.

The Emotionally Repressed Male (ERM)

Above all, this message is to my Brothers in Anger. I know your pain — the unresolved grief of childhood that you carry around inside. I also share your shame — the shame of knowing that you yell, throw things, and hit your partner and/or children. I've felt your rage and I've felt your sorrow after each blow-up.

Now, I've decided to change our label. We've been called wife-beaters and abusers, batterers, or even misogynists. Clinically we are diagnosed as having a type of personality disorder, such as antisocial or narcissistic. After careful consideration, I've come up with a new term that better defines us ... The **Emotionally Repressed Male**, or **ERM** for short.

ERMs can be considered normal and even excel in many areas of our lives — intelligence, social skills, financial abilities, physical prowess, and even spiritual awareness — and yet be emotional children inside. We use our minds, our wit, our leadership positions, our size, and even our enlightenment to overpower others. We repress and discount our emotions, such as anger, jealousy, fear, or sadness.

Inside, however, bottled-up feelings of rage are bubbling and periodically exploding. We cover these feelings with addictions and cover these addictions with denial. "They do not exist!" Externally we put on a great show; internally we are out of control. Being internally out of control, we feel the need to control our environment, becoming selfish and manipulative and unfeeling toward others.

Indeed, we can't "feel" at all, except our own pain which we've denied and numbed. And denying our pain numbs us to the grief we cause others. As we learned from our parents, we continue the tradition of abuse with our families unless there is intervention.

I hope you will read the remainder of this book. I've searched my entire adult life for these answers. I consider them to be of great worth. If you are tired of living with your abusive behavior, now is the time to begin to heal emotionally.

Robert Robertson

PART ONE

The Problem, Source, And Price Of Abusive Behavior

What is the difference between anger and abusive behavior? Where do they originate and what prices to we pay for them? Recognizing these questions and obtaining their answers brought me out of denial and started me on the road to recovery.

This section will discuss:
 – the differences between anger and abuse
 – the role of denial
 – how abusive behavior occurs in cycles and why
 – the causes and origins of abusive behavior
 – interpersonal and physiological price paid for this
behavior

Above all, it clearly defines **Emotionally Repressed Males, (ERMs)** — who they are, how they behave, and why they do the things they do, without any apparent regard for other's emotional or physical well being.

Robert Robertson

~ 1 ~

"I DON'T HAVE A PROBLEM!"
(Abusive Behavior and Denial)

John R. sits in front of me, defiantly. It is his first visit to our Thursday night men's group. "I don't want to be here, and I think it is unfair that my wife insist that I go to counseling." The initial call for him to come to counseling was made by an attorney for his wife, who was threatening divorce. "Anyone would be angry with her," he continues. "Besides, I didn't do anything." His wife currently has her arm in a sling after it was sprained during their last argument. "It was an accident... She continued to provoke me until I blew up."

I truly believed my ex-wife caused my anger and abusive behavior. Frequently I would say to myself (or to anyone else who would listen to me), "If only Kate would change, life would be perfect. If she would just do her part — lose weight, keep the house clean, keep the kids quiet — life would be fine. It's not fair that I have to put up with her behavior. She's the reason I'm angry." I would continually extol my own virtues and my patience with her. I was very convincing to everyone who knew us. I had even convinced myself that abuse was necessary — I needed to call her names, kick doors, or threaten her with violence to convince her of her mistakes and to make her listen.

Feelings deep inside of me, however, made me think that

something else was wrong (perhaps with me?). For ten years (until 1982), I had searched for answers, reading every book I could find, before I had finally given up. I had researched everywhere to find out what was causing this rage inside of me. I eventually concluded that I was not at fault and that Kate was the cause of my misery. That was unfortunate because the answers to all my questions started to appear in the mid-1980's. Had I continued my search I could have saved my marriage. Indeed, I now know that instead of Kate being the cause of my anger, I was the cause of her behavior with which I was unhappy.

What Is Anger?

Anger can be defined as an emotion, or feeling, that is usually secondary to a primary feeling that is being masked, such as grief, shame or some other internal pain. Anger by itself is neither bad nor good. It has a spectrum, usually given on a scale of one to ten, that ranges from mild annoyance to extremely upset.

Mild Annoyance	Upset	Extremely Upset
■■■■■■■■■■■■■■■■■■■■■■■■■■■■■■■■■■■■■■■		
0 Displeased 5 Very Upset 10		

Anger can trigger many different levels of reaction, depending upon the context of the triggering event, the amount of stress one is under, and one's background and personality. I have found there are several situations in which I have to be careful — my "red flag" situations — my worst being when I am driving. I also know that when under a lot of stress I will react differently than others to the same situation. A recent study done with children, some who were abused and others who weren't, shows two different reactions to the same event — getting hit by a snowball. Those from non-abusive homes were likely to think the event accidental, whereas those from abusive homes reacted with anger and hostility. *In the same situation individuals had different reactions, demonstrating that the reality of any event is determined from the inside (one's thinking) and not from the event.*

Myths Of Anger

Matthew McKay, Peter Rogers, and Judith McKay, in their book *When Anger Hurts* (1989, pg 9-20), list four commonly held myths about anger. The first myth is that anger is a biochemically determined event. However, what actually happens is that thinking, not body chemistry, determines anger. Myth number two is that anger and aggression are instinctual to man. They show that different societies (for example, the Japanese) react differently to the same situation. The third myth they dispel is that frustration leads to aggression. Again, not so. We choose to be aggressive. Frustration is a feeling, aggression is a behavior. Myth number four says that it is healthy to ventilate. What happens instead when someone ventilates is not a decrease but an escalation of anger that leads to violence. In other words, research shows all four of these to be untrue and that many times anger and aggression are not necessary. In reality, our thoughts determine our anger.

In doing personal research I have found other myths about anger. For example, many people say, "He or she made me angry, they started it, they made me mad." The answer I give is, "You are angry, period. You are an angry person. You carry a lot of anger around with you, which is really unresolved grief and negative inner voices in your head. You may get into a situation that stimulates you to anger but the reaction is your choice. No one makes you angry."

Another myth I hear people affirm is, "It takes two to argue." My response is, "Sorry, it may take two people to argue but either one of them can take a time-out, choose to walk away or choose not to escalate and not to be abusive."

The third myth is, "Well that's the way I am. It works. It usually settle arguments." The questions I have them ask themselves are, "How well has it worked for you so far? Has it worked in the long run?" It may work in the short run, but in the long run it usually ruins relationships.

Still another myth is, "They were out to get me." My reply: "That is not true. No one is out to get you. Don't take it personally. People usually don't know who you are or care that much about you to want to be out to get you." This is especially true when someone is driving or is having other contact with strangers.

The fifth myth is, "I wasn't angry and abusive. I may have appeared that way but I was under control." My remark to that is, "In reality you have minimized the problem. Just because you didn't call it 'anger' doesn't mean it wasn't and you probably terrified your partner."

The sixth myth is, "I've tried to change but I can't." To this I say, "That is the big lie. Others have changed and so can you but you must be willing to pay the price to change before anything can happen." These prices leading to change include emotional pain, the financial cost of counseling, and time away from other activities. They are essential to recovery.

Reactions To Anger

What do we do when we get angry? Usually, if we don't know how to be assertive, we mishandle our anger in one of three ways. We may stuff it away and suppress it. When someone does that they usually blow up later. I frequently did this and my ex-wife said she used to feel like she was walking around on eggshells, just waiting for me to explode.

Secondly, we sometimes displace our anger. We can direct it away from the source of our anger to another. I owned my own contracting business for ten years. During the day I would get angry at my workmen, but not wanting to displease them so they would not perform, I simply stuffed that anger away and waited until I got home and took it out on my wife.

The third thing we do when we mishandle our anger is to behave in an abusive manner.

The Four Types Of Abusive Behavior

Anger is a feeling. Abuse, however, is a behavior. It is a reaction, always inappropriate, to internal anger. There are four types of abusive behavior:

– The first type is **psychological or emotional abuse.** Examples include name-calling and verbal threats. Or, not saying anything but looking at someone in a very threatening manner. This also includes giving the cold shoulder treatment or totally ignoring someone for a period of time. These are all examples of emotional abuse and can differ in severity. Severe emotional abuse can be just as damaging as physical abuse. Intensely angry words can hurt like thrown punches.

> *Bill J. has a favorite name for his wife when he is angry. He knows that it really hurts her and uses it whenever he wants to inflict pain upon her.*

> *Steve M. insists on having his meals served to him alone when he is angry. He'll go for weeks without talking to his wife. Several times he has threatened to leave her. When asked what is wrong he simply says, "Nothing."*

– The second type of abuse involves **pets and property** — kicking the dog or cat, throwing objects, kicking the door, or putting a fist through the wall. This is done to intimidate another or act out frustrations. It is usually an escalation from verbal or emotional abuse and leads to the next type of abuse.

Tom T. had all he could take. He needed to make a point. Without saying a word, he picks up a dirty dish and throws it against the wall. The shattered pieces fly all over the room. His wife stops talking and looks at him with a shocked expression.

Gary A. had a bad day at work. He walks into the house and at once notices that the family dog has strewn the contents of the garbage can all over the floor. In a fit of anger, he kicks the dog.

– The third type of abuse is **physical abuse**. It not only means hitting someone but also includes pushing, grabbing, pulling hair, twisting an arm, or doing anything that inflicts physical pain.

Rick S. decides he isn't getting his point across to his wife. He grabs her by her hair and points her toward the "mistake" she has made. "Here, stupid, is what I am talking about."

Bob M.'s wife, in making a point, points her index finger at him. To retaliate, Bob grabs her finger and twists it backwards. She spends the next two hours in the emergency ward of the hospital.

– Fourth, and lastly, is **sexual abuse**, such as forced sexual activity upon another person and/or the use of derogatory sexual comments uttered for the express purpose of intimidation.

Bill S. forces his wife to perform sex acts she does not enjoy. He ignores her pleas and threatens to withhold household money if she does not comply. He also calls her sexually insulting names.

Terry P. believes his wife is having an affair with the neighbor. Once, during an argument, she leaves and goes to the neighbor's house for the night. When Terry finds her, he kicks down the door, tears off her clothes, and inspects her to see if she has been faithful.

Not only are these actions morally reprehensible but most are illegal. The purpose is to lower the self-esteem of the victim and gain control. *I would highly recommend immediate help if you are involved in an abusive relationship where there has been severe emotional abuse or any physical or sexual abuse.*

I'll never forget the first time I heard about these four types of abuse. I had just learned this information from reading a book on abuse and violence. It was already too late in my relationship. My wife had a Ryder truck, filled with her belongings, parked in front of our house. In two days she was moving out of state with our children.

I had humbled myself enough to recognize that I did have a problem and then found a counselor in town who dealt with anger and abusive relationships. I talked Kate, my wife, into going to the initial session with me, even though she was leaving the next day. As the counselor explained these four types of abuse, I remember Kate nodding and saying, "Yes, he is guilty of that" and giving details. I began to realize that I had been guilty of all four types of abuse. I couldn't believe it. I had denied and minimized the problem for so long that I had begun to believe the problem didn't exist. Now I was hearing it and knew that it was true. My days of denial were over.

The Emotionally Repressed Male (ERM)

As stated in the introduction, I have coined a term to better describe an abusive male — the Emotionally Repressed Male or ERM. Although normal or even exceptional in areas such as intellect, social skills, physical abilities, business skills, or even spirituality, ERMs are repressed emotionally — a three-year-old in an adult body. ERMs capitalize on their strengths (size and knowledge) and are usually successful at what they are trying to achieve.

However, the storm within (unresolved childhood pain caused by abuse) usually rages and peaks periodically, unleashing the wrath of a three-year-old with an adult body on an unsuspecting and mostly innocent bystander. When he is not "acting out" angrily, his pain of unresolved childhood grief is covered with layers of addictions. Drugs, alcohol, sex, and "living in your head" are prominent addictions, but there could be many others. These addictions are covered with a thick shell of denial.

Eight Characteristics Of Emotionally Repressed Males (ERMs)

#1 – ERMs have **low self-esteem** but are very good at covering that fact with externals. Even though my self-esteem was low, I put on a good act. I had a good business, I was successful in my church, I had a good physical appearance and a wonderful family. And I used all those things to project the image of myself as a great person.

#2 – ERMs are **isolated**, especially from male friends, yet seem to be normal or even excel socially. I was emotionally isolated from close friendships, but I had many so-called acquaintances who really did not know me. This isolation was self-imposed because I was ashamed of others finding out what I was "really like." I was able to control my public appearance at the expense of my family. When Kate decided to separate from me, everyone was in a complete state of shock. They couldn't believe she was going to leave such a perfect husband. Everyone was convinced that she was making a big mistake.

#3 – ERMs are extremely **co-dependent**. They are jealous, they are fearful, and these emotions know no boundaries. Before I married Kate I told her she was going to be my mom and dad ...that she was going to be my whole life. Only now do I realize how unhealthy that statement was.

#4 – ERMs tend to be **self-centered** and experience no guilt from the incidents of abuse they instigate; instead they feel justified in their reaction. By denying the pain of their childhood, they deny themselves all tender feelings, including loving and accepting others. They are judgmental and negative and critical. And controlling!

#5 – ERMs tend to have **addictive personalities**. They are susceptible to drugs, alcohol and other addictions, such as sex or food. Cognitive addictions, such as being judgmental or critical or being a perfectionist, are also common. Although at an early age I quit drinking alcohol and smoking cigarettes, until recently I found myself acting out in other ways. I didn't even consider that these behaviors were addictions.

#6 – ERMs usually have a **history of family violence** and poor relationships with their families, especially their fathers. My father was both abusive and neglectful. He never paid any attention to me when I was behaving correctly. Only when I was misbehaving, such as when I left my bike in the yard, would I get any attention. This "attention" was severe physical abuse. All communication with my father could be categorized as emotional abuse. To him, criticizing me was the best way to motivate me.

#7 – ERMs are **controlling** and they use the four types of violence to control their partners. We have a saying in our group, "When you are internally out of control, you try to externally control your environment." That is, when you have raging voices inside your head and nothing inside seems to make sense, you try to control and order everything that goes on around you.

#8 – ERMs are **experts at denial and deceit**. They will blame anyone and everyone for their problems and minimize their behavior. They may even conveniently forget the abuse they have inflicted. I lied to myself so many times I really began to believe it. With 20/20 hindsight it is now easy to see my problem. Before recovery, however, when I wore the thick dark lenses of denial, all appeared "under control."

Partners Of ERMs

What is the abused partner like? At first she blames herself and tries harder, but soon realizes that it is impossible to please her partner. She then begins to experience frustration, grief, depression, and can deteriorate into poor health. There is a gradual deterioration of her self-esteem and self-image. She becomes withdrawn, feels trapped in a situation which she doesn't know how to deal with. Like her partner, she may deny the problem — clinging to the illusion of outward appearances and hoping that there will be a spontaneous remission of the abuse.

Gradually, love for him will be replaced by fear and hatred. She will finally lose all hope of any solution and will stay in the relationship only because of the children, fear of poverty, fear of retaliation or because she has no idea of what else to do. Eventually, out of desperation, she will leave him or somehow terminate the relationship.

Experts At Denial And Deceit

Both abuser and abused are experts at denial. There are several reasons for this. For the abusers, the main reason is that they are trying to defend themselves against emotional pain. The greater the unresolved childhood grief, that is, the greater the abuse they suffered as children, the greater the amount of anger and addictions they use to cover the pain. I know that now. During my own recovery, as I went through the grieving stage, I cried for a full year and a half over my experiences as a child. It became crystal clear to me why I was so filled with anger and how I used my many addictions to conceal — from others, to be sure, but mostly from myself — all those early humiliating experiences. By denying the anger and addictions, I denied the pain.

Another reason that ERMs and their partners are in denial is that they have loyalty to family and family rules, especially the "don't talk, don't feel and don't trust" rule. Family systems are very powerful. I remember when I was twelve years old, my grandmother moved into our home to take care of our family after my mother died. Once she threatened me with a shotgun to get me to behave. I told the next door neighbor about the incident and he told his mother. After his mother talked to my grandmother, I was confronted and told in no uncertain terms that we didn't discuss our personal problems outside the house and I was severely punished. I was also told that what I said wasn't true. I suddenly heard my grandmother saying that she had not done what she had done. I began to deny my own senses and those things that were happening around me.

The third reason for denial is to protect the ERM's low self-esteem. Denying his inner weaknesses and abusive behavior allows him to present to others a facade of respectability. Because he has been plagued with low self-esteem his entire life, he craves acceptance and respect. This behavior tends to promote vanity and self-centeredness.

The fourth reason is that denial does have a purpose. It is part of the healing process. It is a natural and automatic mechanism for coping with grief and tragedy. I have a friend who was in a severe plane wreck and it took her nearly a year to go through the emotional, as well as physical, healing. At first she was in denial and shock and said everything was okay; gradually she was able to express anger; finally, she began to grieve. She then was able to accept what had happened to her. ERMs are stuck in denial of their pain, and it is not good for them to hold on to that denial. The first step in recovery is to eliminate denial, since you cannot work on a problem that you won't admit you have.

Denial in abusive behavior isn't an event but a learned process that progresses very slowly. It is said that if you put a frog into hot water it will jump out immediately. If you put the same frog into cold water and slowly turn up the temperature to boiling, the frog will stay in until it is dead. It is the same with denial. It doesn't happen all at once, but slowly builds up until you can look outside and see the sunshine and say that it is dark.

There are several types of denial:

– The first type is known as **minimizing**. For example, one might say, "I didn't hit her, I simply pushed her." He minimizes the problem to where it doesn't even exist.

– In the second type of denial, the abuser **blames others**. "You made me mad, it is your fault this happened." He fails to take responsibility for his own actions.

– The third type is **rationalization**. He says, after he becomes abusive, "This was necessary; I needed to control the situation; it was getting out of hand." In reality, he is denying the fact that he cannot control himself.

– The fourth type is **total denial**. "What are you talking about?" The next day he conveniently forgets everything that happened.

Recovery

Sooner or later the abuser needs to make a choice. He can continue to act out angrily or he can change. Either way there are prices to be paid. To admit that he is wrong means that he must go through some temporary grief and some temporary sorrow to begin the journey to recovery. However, greater prices will be paid if he continues protecting himself by denying the problem. The beginning of change is admitting there is a problem. It is a humbling experience but one that is better begun by his own volition than to be forced into it by others.

If you recognize yourself in any of the above descriptions of ERMs, then it is definitely time to confront your problem. To make that decision will be difficult, but it will be infinitely more difficult and costly if you wait.

~ 2 ~

"I PROMISE IT WON'T HAPPEN AGAIN"

(Cycles of Abusive Behavior)

Approximately every six months, James C. calls me. "Bob, I need to get into an anger group. My anger is getting really bad again." He works nights as a bartender and cannot make the regular evening sessions. I make special arrangements for a day group and call him one month later to tell him of the time. He says, "Everything is okay now. I guess it was a false alarm. I really don't think I need to work on my problem." I cancel the session. Five months later he calls again seeking help. This has happened three times.

Looking back, I am sure that I was abusive to my wife from the beginning of our marriage until the end. Still, at the end of each abusive episode, convinced that it would never happen again, I promised Kate that I would "control" my temper. My anger always returned, however, and the abuse worsened as time passed. For a while Kate believed me and tried harder to please me. But soon she gave up and separated herself from me, both emotionally and physically.

The Cycle Of Abusive Behavior

The cycle that I am describing, which was first discovered by

Lenore E. Walker in her book, *The Battered Woman* (1979, pg 55-70), is one of the most interesting phenomena about the ERM's abusive behavior. Cycles vary in time and severity, but they are present in almost all abusive behavior. Kate said I had a perfect six-month cycle for the first ten years of our marriage but it shortened and became more intense the last two years we were together.

The cycle of abusive behavior has three phases:

– The first phase is called the **build-up phase**. During this time feelings are stuffed away and the voices in your head (the so-called negative "self-talk," which we will discuss in Chapter Eight) can drive you crazy. This phase is fed by stress. The more stress you are under, the shorter the phase lasts, and the more severe the abuse that follows. The partner of an ERM can sense the tension and sometimes describes it as "like walking on eggshells." She may try to please and understand her partner but cannot. This phase can last anywhere from days to several years. It is like a pressure cooker (the ERM) being placed over an open flame (the stress) without a release valve (an acceptable outlet). Sooner or later he explodes!

– Then comes phase two or the **blow-up phase**. Here ERMs act out abusively, using one or more of the four types of abuse. Many times the ERM's partner feels she was the cause. In reality, no matter what she does, it is "never enough" nor is she ever "right." Kate would try to do everything right but I would always find something to blow up about. I didn't actually need anything to blow up about — I needed to get rid of the stress and that was the reason I acted angrily and abusively. Phase two can last anywhere from five minutes to all day. It, too, is much worse when the abuser is under severe stress. It can be very severe when the abuser is under the influence of drugs or alcohol. It only stops when the stress has been abated or the abuser is afraid because something is destroyed, someone is injured, or because the police may be called.

– After the second phase is over the third phase begins. It is called the **make-up phase**. Here ERMs feel remorse for their behavior and act very loving. They promise "never again" and they can be very convincing! It is this phase and behavior that generally keeps the relationship together and keeps both partners in denial. He enjoys being relieved of the inner stress. She desperately hopes that it will never happen again and enjoys the special attention. After several such cycles, however, she knows her hopes were unfounded.

What exactly is this cycle of abuse? What we are witnessing is the first three steps of the grieving cycle — denial, anger, and bargaining. (This was first discussed by Elisabeth Kübler-Ross in her book, *Death-The Final Stage of Growth*, 1975). However, ERMs, upon reaching the next phase, which is grief, quickly drop back into denial. The grief phase is painful. Old unresolved childhood pains are dredged up from memory (more of this in Chapter Fourteen). Rather than face those pains, ERMs quickly re-cover them with addictions and denial. By hoping for a miracle (a form of "magical thinking"), ERMs pretend that nothing has happened and restart the cycle of abusive behavior. Instead of dealing with the pain and associated abuse, they pretend they don't exist.

Myths Disproved By Cycle

This cycle disproves three commonly held myths:

– The first myth is that men want to be abusive. I think that the cycle shows that in reality they don't want to be abusive. Phase one (the build-up phase) shows a desire to control their behavior. ERMs stuff their feelings in desperate hope of controlling their actions. However, like the pressure cooker without a valve, sooner or later they explode (phase two — the blow-up phase). Almost all treatment for ERMs is directed at phase one behavior. Once in phase two the only thing they can do is take a time-out (see Chapter Six).

– The second myth is that men are only abusive with their families. Ask police officers what the most dangerous call to which they must respond is. They will probably tell you that it is a domestic argument. When ERMs are in phase two, they seldom can control their behavior and are likely to hit or strike out at anyone within reach.

Prior to my recovery, one of the greatest fears I had was that during this phase, I would do something very violent. One such fearful episode occurred when I was in the Army. I had just finished NCO (Non-Commissioned Officers) School and was going through the second part of that training. I was assigned to a platoon with another sergeant (a "lifer") who was on permanent duty there. He had angry feelings towards me because I was an NCO candidate (he had fifteen more years service and only one more stripe) and because I had been to military school and knew quite a bit about drill and ceremony. I suppose he was jealous of me and I'm sure my attitude didn't help either.

An opportunity arose for him to show his superior knowledge and make me look foolish. We were on a course called "Escape and Evasion" and I had to lead my squad of men through a ten-mile area at night. There was an opposing force along the way, made up of his men, who were trying to capture us. He offered anyone a reward who was able to capture me specifically. If anyone got caught, they could legally be tortured. It was very realistic training and I deeply feared what would happen to me if I were to be captured. I knew that I would get so mad that I would probably try to kill the sergeant. Fortunately, we avoided capture. Everytime I read about an act of violence in the newspaper, although I don't approve, I understand what happened.

–The third myth is that the abusive behavior will stop with phase three. ERMs are very convincing, yet always will recycle this behavior without treatment. The partner needs to practice tough love and insist that the abuser get help. Most important, she must stick to that decision, whatever the cost. The longer these cycles continue without intervention — the build-up, the blow-up, the make-up — the worse they'll get.

Without treatment, what happens over time is:

– phase one (the build-up) shortens

– phase two (the blow-up) becomes more violent and lasts for longer periods of time

– phase three (make-up) shortens and eventually disappears.

If you were to graph the level of violence over a period of time the graph would look like this:

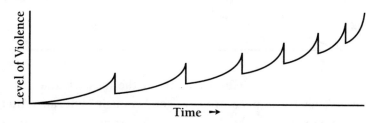

What About The Abused?

I also noticed a corresponding graph or cycle for the person who was being abused. The chief difference between the two graphs is that the abused weren't able to fully recover. It is the cycle that I went through as a child, and that ERMs put their partners through as adults. Practically everyone will go through this cycle as they unconsciously develop their abusive behavior.

Tension rises for both the abuser and the abused in the first phase. When abused during the second phase, the abused person's tension continues to rise, because he/she is not allowed to relieve the stress caused by the abuser.

While children, ERMs were not allowed to talk or fight back. Such was my experience. I had no outlet for my anger or grief and, as a result, all the unresolved emotions became the impetus for the rage released during my phase two (blow-up) behavior as an adult.

ERMs insist that their partners conform to their arbitrary rules. In many ways, I believe some partners "allow" this cycle to continue due to their own co-dependent needs. They feel that even an unsafe familiar environment is better than a safe unfamiliar one.

Each progressive step or cycle of abuse causes a corresponding increase in stress. The graph looks like this:

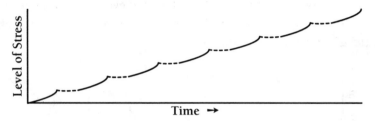

Over time three events occur. At first the abused blame themselves. They try desperately to be "good enough," but can't. After more time and abuse, they have an emotional separation from their partners. Even though they may feel they are guilty, they separate themselves emotionally from the abuser in an attempt to protect their feelings. Finally, there comes rebellion and a physical separation, and they may even become abusive themselves in order to release their own stress.

I remember that Kate went through each of these phases in our marriage. She said that at first she very much blamed herself and thought she just had to try harder to please me. She soon realized that nothing she did was enough. She then began to separate herself from me emotionally. Finally, she reached the point where she no longer felt safe around me. We had an actual physical separation twice and finally the divorce.

Women who have gone through this cycle must remember that they have been trained, like their partners, to become abusive. This is why women continue to "act out" angrily after being in abusive relationships and must be allowed to vent those feelings in a safe environment. They must grieve over the pain to which they have been exposed or it will continue to be recycled to others, just as their partners recycled their childhood pain to them.

Storing Pain for Later Abuse

I remember in my own life when my dad had been abusive to me. I was never allowed to express my feelings; thus I was never able to fully recover. His favorite line was, "I'll give you something to cry about."

One time, when my dad was in his make-up stage (phase three) and feeling remorse for being abusive, he bought me a go-cart. He proudly opened up the trunk of the car to show it to me. It was packed in a large brown cardboard box. As I looked into the trunk, all I could see was a box with two metal packing straps around it. He asked me what I thought. I looked up at him and asked him, "Are you going to beat me with those metal straps?" I still felt like I was very bad and needed to be punished more.

After being abused as a child, I never could recover fully the way my father could. By not being allowed to vent my feelings, I stuffed them deeply away, only to have them surface at a later date. Each time they surfaced, it was like a ravenous wolf that had been trapped in a cage and had finally clawed its way free. Each resurfacing was more violent and terrifying than the one before.

I did not know what to do.

~ 3 ~

"WHY DO YOU TREAT ME THIS WAY?"

(Origins of Abusive Behavior)

It is Tuesday night's group and Charlie P. is talking about his relationship with his wife. "At first she didn't complain. She did what I said. It seemed to work. Then things began to go crazy. She began to fight with me. It continues to get worse." He admits to problems at work, stress because of finances, and a history of family abuse and alcholism with his parents. "But, I know that doesn't affect me now. I think the real reason for my problem is my wife's new attitude. She is fighting back. Things were okay when she listened to me."

If you listen to an ERM, he'll try to convince you his abuse is justified or that his partner is totally at fault for his abusive behavior. My famous line to Kate was, "You screwed up, I got mad, and suddenly all we talk about is my anger." I was firmly convinced that she was the source of all of my problems and the solution was for her to change.

Now, of course, I know that is nonsense. Abused women are not masochistic. They do not ask for trouble nor do they go looking for it. They also don't deserve the treatment they receive. In retrospect I realize that Kate was a saintly woman for putting up with me for as long as she did.

Five Reasons For Abusive Behavior

ERMs are abusive for several reasons, *none* of which have anything to do with their partner's looks, performance, personality, beliefs or reactions.

The first is **control**: ERMs have a need to control other people. Many have not learned boundaries in their own lives, and controlling others comes naturally. For an ERM, controlling everything, to a degree, does lessen stress. As stated before, when someone is out of control internally, they have a desire to control others, to put things in order externally. In the short term it may be effective in some relationships, but over the long term it almost always destroys them.

> *Pete M. is a demanding boss who always needs to be in charge. He lists tasks each day for his wife and family before he goes to work. Each person is expected to have his/her list completed when he gets home or pay "the price."*

The second reason ERMs are abusive is because **it works**! Anger and abuse appear to get them what they want. They don't know how to use other types of behavior, such as assertiveness (See Chapter Ten), to fulfill their needs. They are either passive (stuff their feelings) or aggressive (blow up). They have a hammer (their anger) and all their problems resemble nails. Again, in the short term it may appear to work, but it almost always destroys, given enough time.

> *Aaron P. has tried unsuccessfully to convince his wife to stop arguing with him. Finally, in a fit of rage, he slams his fist on the table. She stops talking.*

The third reason ERMs are abusive is to **relieve stress**. For example, they may build up a lot of stress at work and then blow up at home. They know of no healthy outlet for getting rid of that stress. I know that at the end of our arguments I would feel great but my wife felt destroyed.

When I became single again, I dated a woman who once was verbally abusive to me. When it was over she said she felt relieved and felt much closer to me. To me, it was like a punch in the stomach. I never wanted to see her again. Many ERMs are isolated and need to have an outlet to rid themselves of stress. That is why I feel group counseling is so effective. It allows association with other men and also allows the relief of stress in a positive manner, through group discussion.

John S. had a rotten day at work. As he drives home, he can hear the engine of his car knocking and knows that it is time for a valve job. When he arrives at his house, he sees toys all over the yard where his kids have been playing. He begins to yell at them about all that he does for his family. They stand silently by and listen to his tirade.

A fourth reason for being abusive is that ERMs were **taught** to be that way. They learned abuse from their roles within the family and the stereotypes on TV and in the movies. Invariably, it is the wrong picture there. Many television shows and movies depict two types of men: wimpy nerds or strong he-man types who tend to be controlling and abusive. Of course, male children choose the latter for their role model. Women are also stereotyped as desiring to be treated that way, succumbing to the abusive behavior in a masochistic way. Art seldom imitates life in Hollywood.

Mark J. believes real men don't let women get away with anything. He is still trying to find a woman who will appreciate one of the last frontier men. "I was born too late," he sadly laments.

However, the **main reason** men are abusive is because they were **abused as children**. Stored memories of ungrieved pain from childhood abuse serve as the source of current feelings of rage. These memories are the single most important factor in determining just how abusive an ERM will eventually become. As children, ERMs learned unhealthy coping skills (don't talk, don't trust, and especially don't feel) to survive the abuse meted out by their caregivers. At the time, these skills were essential to survival. But, they are inappropriate in adults and are detrimental to healthy relationships.

As discussed in Chapter Two, these men stuffed their feelings of rage without grieving them through. They became ERMs. They learned not to feel anything, including remorse, for their behavior toward others. They continued their abuse even though they knew it to be wrong. *It is not enough to "know" when they are doing wrong, they must be able to "feel" the pain that they inflict upon others.*

My Own Training Ground

One of my older sisters told me of many situations in my childhood when I was abused as an infant. She said that I was a colicky baby and was shaken by my father many times to "punish" me, or to make me quit crying and go to sleep. I learned to rock myself to sleep by hitting my head against the headboard, similar to an autistic child. It was probably the only way I felt comfort (loved?) enough to go to sleep.

When I was a year old my father decided he would teach me how to walk. He stood me up in the middle of the living room and he sat down on the couch with his arms outstretched. When I fell down, he came over, stood me up, and tried it again. My two older sisters were watching. My mother wasn't home. After I fell down several times, he became disgusted with me, pulled my diaper down, and spanked me severely.

My sisters became terrified and began screaming for me to get up and try to walk. One of my sisters tried to help but was told to stop. All I could do was sit on the floor and cry. I didn't want to go to him. Even at the early age of one year, I was terrified of my dad. He spanked me several more times (my sister said approximately six times).

Finally, he gave up because my sisters were behaving hysterically. They were crying, "Get up, Bobby. Please get up." When my mother came home and changed my diaper, she noticed that I had welts on my bottom. She never left me alone with my dad again!

Most of the early episodes of abuse in my childhood have been forgotten but I distinctly remember fearing my dad. The first instance of abuse I clearly remember was when I was seven years old. I hadn't seen my dad for several months — he had been out of state on business. When he came home that night I was so excited to see him that, without thinking, I pulled my bicycle behind his car and ran into the house. Later that evening, as he left with my mom, he backed his car over my bike. He came back inside, and with a look of rage on his face, pulled his belt off and began to whip me severely until I had belt markings.

Another time, I was getting ready for church on Easter Sunday. We were going to have a family picture taken in our new clothes before we left. I wasn't getting ready fast enough so my mom decided that we would not go to the early service but would go later in the day. My dad went into a fit of rage and spanked me severely. He jerked me outside by the back of my neck and made me have my picture taken. I will always remember that picture. My coat was on crooked, I was standing at attention, and my hands were straight out.

Recently I re-examined that picture. I was only seven years old when it was taken. At the time I was examining the picture, my oldest son was seven years old. I suddenly came to the realization that my son was incapable of being a bad boy, as bad as I thought I was at the time that picture was taken. Yet I bought the belief that I was bad hook, line and sinker. I didn't simply behave badly — I "was bad."

What was really happening that Easter Sunday, when I was a child, was that my dad was having an affair with a woman who lived up the street. My not being ready to go on time cut into his time with her. He was unable to see her that day because of the change in church schedule. He took out his frustration on me. Because of these and many similar incidents, my dad and I never had a close relationship. As a matter of fact, I had not spoken to him for several years before his death. He made a point of telling everyone not to notify me in the event of his death, so I was unable to attend his funeral.

I learned my lessons well. I learned to use manipulative be-havior, put-downs that cut to the core, looks that destroyed con-fidence and esteem, and threatening behavior that terrified those who received it. I acted out forcefully because I had a powerful teacher and I was his star student. For a time in my life, my dad was everything in my eyes. He was very successful. He was a self-made millionaire. He was recognized as being the outstanding person in his state in 1967. He was in *Who's Who*. He also was a womanizer who kept as many as six woman on a string at a time.

I wanted to be just like him. He was my hero. Although there was a time in high school when I acted out in rebellion against his control, I later found myself acting just like him in my marriage.

As a child I was very dependent upon my mom. She was the only source of love that I can remember. I felt abandoned when she died in a car accident when I was twelve years old. The fear of abandonment continued to contaminate me as an adult. I became as dependent upon my wife as I had been on my mother and was terrified of being abandoned by her. I wanted to control her so she would never leave me. Instead, my control and abuse drove her away.

What a great price I had to pay to break out of denial and examine and change my behavior!

The author, at age one, when "taught" to walk by his father.

The Easter picture, age seven.

Robert Robertson

~ 4 ~

"THIS ISN'T FAIR!"
(Prices Paid for Abusive Behavior)

Pam P. talks hesitantly about her past marriage. "I really loved Rick and appreciated all that he did, but the abuse was killing me. It overshadowed all the nice things he did for us. Sure, he was a great provider, the kids loved him, and most of the time we got along great. But towards the end, all I could think of was the abuse... The waiting for him to blow up... The fear of what he would do next. I had to get out." Her husband, Rick, is in a state of shock. Not only did his wife leave and take his kids but he was served with a restraining order that prevented him from seeing them. Only a week before, he had lost his job of eight years. Within six months, his health has deteriorated, he stays home most nights alone, he is unable to find work, and he loses his house in a foreclosure. "This isn't fair!"

During our last winter together as a couple, I reflected upon my personal and family life and my financial position. Kate and I had been in our new home for about three years. Business was really great, I was busy serving my church, and was very happy with my personal life in general, or so I thought. The only thing that I thought needed to change was my wife, Kate. I reasoned that I needed a slim attractive wife who kept a neat house. Of course, I now realize I was deep in denial of the real problem.

We separated the first time that spring. She took the kids with her to visit her dad, who was having back problems. That gave her a good excuse to leave without anyone knowing that we were separated, and also gave her time to be alone. Time, I thought, for her to "clean up her act." Now I realize it was a time for her to think about what she wanted to do next with our relationship.

As I was home alone that summer, I reflected on the years that Kate and I had shared. I remembered the first time I saw Kate. Her appearance was stunning and I was smitten when I began talking to her. I said to myself, "The guy who marries her will be the luckiest man in the world." We married my last year of college.

I remembered some of our financial struggles. The last three months in college, which were during the summer while I was working on my Master's thesis, we didn't even have enough money to eat. I'll always remember the look of great joy on my wife's face when I came home with groceries one afternoon after being paid for a part-time job. She was about three months pregnant and had not had anything to eat for a week but my Boy Scout bread (flour, water, sugar, baking soda, salt) and baked beans. She started to cry and I held her in my arms for a long time.

After I graduated from college, we moved to Florida and I started working at a job in industrial sales. Those were happy times. After our son was born, I can remember taking him to the pool in back of the apartment complex where we lived and teaching him, as an infant, how to swim. Surrounding the apartments was a concrete walk way beside a canal where we took evening walks. It was a pretty place to live.

One year later, we moved to the West Coast, so I could attend a professional program at school. I also started my own contracting business. We struggled along for five or six years. We lived in a house next door to a man who had a very smelly furnace. He collected old metal and wire, burned off the insulation, and resold it. Our own house had holes in the floor when we first moved there. Finally we moved into a nice, spacious house and everything was going well.

Kate returned home in the fall and left for good the next spring.

As I think about it, the financial struggles we had left very fond memories. It was my abuse that killed the relationship. I had behaved toward my family the same way my dad had behaved toward me. Even though I was never happy as a child, it was the only behavior I knew. I'm still compiling a list of all the prices I paid for my abusive behavior. I am sure that it will not be complete for years to come. I have divided the prices into two types: **physiological and interpersonal.**

Physiological Prices

My wife paid a heavy physiological price because of the abuse I heaped upon her. She had periods of depression. It even changed her menstrual cycle, and she had a general lack of energy. My abuse not only failed to solve the problems that I was always harping at her about, but it made them worse. The house was messier, she was unhappy, and she gained weight.

I didn't start my own physiological suffering until after she left. When I suddenly realized that it was over and I was out of denial, I experienced a lot of physical pain. I had fits of crying spells, my stomach ached, and I was mentally confused. I even discovered that there were big holes in my fingernails caused by all the worry and stress I was under.

I had a picture taken the summer we were separated and another a short time after the divorce — a before and after picture (they were I.D. photos). I could not believe how devastated my appearance had become. It took over two years to overcome that look.

Anger, in general, can be very damaging to certain types of people. It can cause and increase the severity of heart disease, high blood pressure, ulcers, and a host of other illnesses. Your angry thoughts can literally kill you. I was fortunate that I personally didn't suffer from any of these.

Interpersonal Prices

By far, the greatest price I paid was the interpersonal price. We had a great love in our marriage at first. It distanced, then ceased, then she moved away. I have not only lost my wife but I have lost my children, as they now live with her in another state. I call them weekly and visit them three or four times a year but they are no longer here. They also paid a great price by watching the violent behavior between their mother and father.

Financially it has set me back several years. I have to pay a large amount of child support and I have to pay taxes now as a single person. The cost of our divorce wiped out all our investments and put me in debt. My business suffered, as I was unable to concentrate on anything but my own problems, and my income dropped by one-third over the next two years.

There have been many personal problems as well. I had to put together a new social life. I lacked any motivation to work around the house or do anything that was not absolutely necessary. My self-respect plummeted. Most of all, I now realize that anger and abuse is met with anger and abuse. Whether you are driving or doing business or any other thing, whenever you are angry and abusive that is the type of behavior you get back. You definitely reap what you sow.

There Must Be A Better Way

When I was a teenager, I attended military school. In the infirmary there was a nurse who made everyone gargle hot salt water when they were sick. It was a great source of amusement to all the cadets. We would jokingly say that, if someone came in with a broken arm, she'd say, "Here, go gargle with this hot salt water." Well, that is the way my anger was. Every time I was confronted by anyone for any reason, I responded with anger. I had to pay a great price to learn a valuable lesson: there was a better way to deal with others.

If you are an abuser, I'm sure that if you were to compile your own list of physiological and interpersonal prices, you would see that your anger is not worth the price. You may think right now that you would be better off without your spouse, but this feeling would change dramatically if circumstances were to change.

Kate once asked me if I would rather have a clean house or a house with kids. At first I thought a clean house would be best, yet I now realize the foolishness of that belief. I've cried many, many times in my clean empty house. I'd walk into my daughter's room and look at her dollhouse sitting there untouched and burst into tears. I'd go downstairs to my son's room and see the things that I had given him, such as my scout momentos, and grieve, knowing that I am not with him to share this time of his life.

The prices continue today. Right now we are having a dispute over divorce terms, kid's visits, living places, and other things. I am sure these differences will continue for a long time. Kate said at the end that she could no longer trust me with her feelings. Only after I got in touch with my own feelings could I realize what she meant.

ERMs cannot feel, but it is not because they are without feelings. They have simply lost contact with them. All of the unresolved childhood grief which they now carry covers up the innocent child that they once were. This childhood grief was covered over with addictions, and the addictions were then covered over with denial.

My self-centeredness around my own pain caused me to ignore Kate's pain. Getting in touch with my feelings made me realize what I had done to her. I now realize that I have lost a wonderful wife. Now I am able to see the whole picture.

When I look back over the years and remember my college sweetheart — the first date we had, being there to witness our children's births, our financial struggles and successes — I realize that all of those things are now just painful memories, clouded with the other memories of abusive actions that I perpetrated against her.

I hope that I have painted a vivid picture here and that it serves to motivate abusers to change. If you are one, I'm sure you can compile your own list of prices that your anger has cost you. If you are motivated, the next section will show you how to begin to change from being an Emotionally Repressed Male into an Emotionally Responsive Male.

PART TWO

Recovery From Abusive Behavior

A good analogy for anger and abusive behavior can be found in a glass of carbonated water. The bubbles represent anger. As the bubbles reach the surface, they explode, just as the inner anger turns into abusive behavior as it surfaces. The intent of treatment, then, is to "attack" the anger at its source, so that the "bubbling up" eventually ceases. Each treatment helps to lessen the amount of anger reaching the surface.

The **twelve steps** of abuse recovery are:

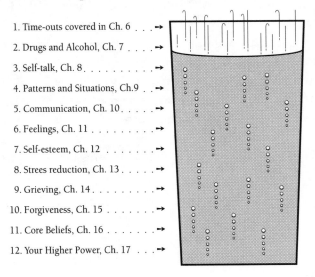

1. Time-outs covered in Ch. 6 . . . ➙

2. Drugs and Alcohol, Ch. 7 . . . . ➙

3. Self-talk, Ch. 8 . . . . ➙

4. Patterns and Situations, Ch.9 . . ➙

5. Communication, Ch. 10 . . . . . ➙

6. Feelings, Ch. 11 . . . . ➙

7. Self-esteem, Ch. 12 . . . . ➙

8. Strees reduction, Ch. 13 . . . . . ➙

9. Grieving, Ch. 14 . . . . ➙

10. Forgiveness, Ch. 15 . . . . ➙

11. Core Beliefs, Ch. 16 . . . . ➙

12. Your Higher Power, Ch. 17 . . . ➙

All twelve steps take place in the context of group, couple, and individual counseling which is covered in Chapter Five. *This book is not intended to be a substitute for counseling. Do not do any of this work without supervision, especially grieving or inner child work.*

There are two generally recognized methods of treatment for abusive males. The first, or the traditional method, treats only the behavior, with emphasis on stopping the violence. The second, and more complete approach, treats not only the behavior but addresses larger issues such as stereotyped roles, equal treatment, and sharing of responsibilities. I believe that if one is expected to fully recover, all issues — violence as well as the stereotyping — must be addressed. I follow an approach dealing with all issues and add to that both grief work and seeking strength from a Higher Power.

Work is required. A lot of work. Before I got better I had to suffer. *The only way out of the pain is through it.* Again, ERMs have a hammer, their anger, to solve their problems, which resemble nails. You really need a complete toolbox. These "tools" include: learning new behaviors, such as assertiveness; recognizing and handling feelings, without letting them become anger; and restructuring core beliefs, thereby obtaining an effective "map" of reality.

You must also do all the required work (exercises or twelve steps), and not simply the reading, to recover. Reading books to achieve recovery is like reading exercise books to improve your body. Without doing the "exercises" the results are non-existent.

Let's begin adding new tools and learning new skills for dealing with others.

~ 5 ~

"WE NEED TO GO
TO A COUNSELOR"
A NEW BEGINNING:
GROUP, COUPLE AND INDIVIDUAL COUNSELING

Ben and Marsha R. are sitting in my office for their initial visit. She begins, "Well, I don't know where to start." Tears begin to form in her eyes. Ben shuffles his feet, looks around nervously, and makes angry comments about her behavior. For new clients, I have a "canned" presentation which discusses the types of abuse, the cycle of abuse, and the twelve steps of recovery. After going through my presentation and asking several questions, I begin: "You've done the right thing... You are on the right track. It is going to be a painful journey but not one that is impossible. Are you both committed?" They both nod their heads in agreement.

You can't recover alone. Sooner or later, when you realize that you need help, you must go to a counselor. This is a very difficult decision to make. Many ERMs have fears of counselors, fears of coming out of denial and explaining their problems to an outsider. Other ERMs agree to go to a counselor just to be manipulative or to please their partners instead of wanting to change their behavior and become healthy. You must realize that choosing the right counselor and being receptive to change are the two most important ingredients for the recovery of ERMs.

I know this all too well from my own experience. Kate and I went to four marriage counselors before we had our final separation. None of them were helpful. Perhaps they were not helpful because I was not teachable; I was still in denial, believing it was my wife's problem. But none of them really knew that much about anger nor about abuse counseling. As I found out too late, *this is a special area and requires a specialist.*

Throwing Money Away

The first person we saw was a marriage and family counselor who Kate chose from the yellow pages. I immediately noticed that she had a messy office and was overweight. I thought to myself, "Well, surely she couldn't help Kate with her problem because those were the two things I was demanding most out of her — to keep the house clean and keep her weight down." Maybe she did have some answers, and maybe she didn't. I don't know. She did talk to me about growing up in a dysfunctional family but she didn't really talk about anything to do with anger. She forcefully stated that it was never okay to be abusive but gave no indications of understanding why I was that way. She said nothing about the types of abuse, cycle of abuse, or the underlying reasons for being abusive. I did not feel safe discussing anything with her. At no time was empathy established.

A year passed before we tried someone else. He had been recommended to us by a couple who had been going to him. (They later divorced!) We went to his house and he showed us video tapes of lectures he had given and then proceeded to give us counsel and tests. Everything was the same for everyone he worked with — tapes, counsel, tests. I'll never forget the time he really acted like a kook by impersonating Satan. He put a sheet of paper over his face and then he raised the paper and pretended he was good and then he lowered the paper and pretended he was evil. It made little sense. He was probably the least competent counselor I have ever encountered.

We tried another person who was also referred to us. On our first visit, Kate proceeded to tell the counselor all the abusive things I had done to her. When Kate had finished, the counselor looked over at me with disgust. She gave me a look that was similar to looking into a spittoon that was half full of spit with a green crust around it. She said, "You did *that* to your wife?" I felt very unsafe and I denied everything at the time. No further counseling was given. She wanted to explain all about her office procedure, about how important it was for us to pay her on time, etc. I couldn't wait to get that $80 out of my pocket and leave.

We went to one last counselor before our final separation. Kate had been seeing him alone, trying to decide whether or not she wanted to leave. I went with her once and he gave me what turned out to be the single worst piece of advice any counselor could give: I needed to *control* my anger. So I did. I stuffed my anger away even more, and the next time I blew up I wanted to kill Kate. Getting rid of anger is not accomplished by "controlling" it, but by getting rid of its causes, as we will later see.

Two Keys To Choosing Your Counselor

There are at least two keys in choosing a counselor. The first is that he or she must have training and knowledge of abuse counseling. There are specialists in any field and, just as a medical doctor can't know everything about medicine, neither can all counselors know everything in treating emotional disorders. Very specific treatment is needed. *This is the single most important key in choosing a counselor.*

Number two, you need someone with empathy. A recovered ERM is probably the best person to serve as a counselor for you. I recommend that men get men counselors and women get women counselors. They talk the same language and will have more empathy and understanding for your problems.

Your Part: Being Receptive

Again, choosing a good counselor is half the solution. The other, and most important half, is that you *must become receptive to change*. You must become *humble*, willing to learn, and accept *responsibility* for your abusive behavior. The problem of abuse lies almost entirely with the ERM.

Let me continue my story of recovery. After going to the fourth counselor and not getting any results, and knowing that my wife was going to be leaving soon, as a last resort I fasted for several days and went up onto a mountain to pray. I received a definite indication that everything would be okay. The next week my son had a gymnastics meet in a small town in our state. After watching his performance, I wandered the streets alone, thinking about what was going on in my life. "Where was the answer for which I had prayed?"

Suddenly, I received a strong impression that I should go into a bookstore and that there I would find a book that would help me with my problem. At that bookstore I bought a book called *Learning to Live Without Violence*. Later I found out that that store is probably the only place in the state that I could have bought that book. The newest edition wasn't even in my hometown yet.

I read the book and recognized my problem. The book clearly explained the types of abuse, the cycle of abuse, and the reasons why we are abusive to our partners. When I returned home I located a treatment center specializing in abusive behavior and met with a counselor. At last I was receiving some answers.

The question I have asked many times is, "Did the first four counselors have the answers, but perhaps I wasn't listening?" I can now honestly say that they did not. No one can specialize in everything. If I had heard even one answer to the question, "Why am I abusive?," I would have recognized my problem. Up until that day of the gymnastics meet, I honestly thought that "the problem" was my wife's, and that I was "reacting" to her problem.

Group Counseling

There are several options in counseling for ERMs, but one of the most important things I can recommend to both ERMs and their partners is to get group counseling first. There are several advantages:

– First, groups are excellent places to share feelings. Many times ERMs are isolated emotionally and there is great comfort in knowing that others share the same problems. Groups can also provide an emotional outlet in regard to current issues you are facing, such as work and family, and grieving about past issues, such as your childhood. I know that when I am in my group I literally see the tensions lift off the men's shoulders as they begin to share their stories. In the beginning they fidget, shuffle their feet, and look at the floor or ceiling. Within half an hour, they begin to loosen up and release the stress that they have been carrying around with them as they become involved in the group.

– The second reason for group counseling is that you can learn from others by the stories they tell. ERMs have a very specific profile and share almost identical traits. Every problem that I've ever had, others in the group have also had. Everyone learns valuable lessons there.

– Third, group counseling is a safe and effective place to be confronted with your abusive behavior. ERMs are many times in denial, and group feedback is better than feedback from one person. Often, in my groups, I have what I call a "reality check," asking each participant for his response to what a particular person is saying. There is almost always a unanimous consent as to what actions the individual needs to take to change his abusive behavior.

– Fourth, group counseling is a good place for instruction. Again, ERMs have their hammers and every problem looks like a nail. Group is a great place to fill a toolbox with new skills. A group leader can give weekly lessons about conquering anger and abuse that help group members improve their skills in dealing with other people.

– Last but not least, it is an excellent place to be good to yourself and to help others. You can brag about your accomplishments and give compliments to others as well. This helps build your self-esteem and assists in your recovery.

Men need to go to group counseling because they need to realize that others have overcome the same problems. Also, they can find male friends there and deal with some manliness issues, such as overcoming poor relationships with their parents, dealing with authority figures, or not having any male friends in their lives. Women also benefit from group counseling by having a safe environment to vent their feelings. They can let go of their frustrations without worrying about suffering further abuse. Most of all, they can overcome their co-dependent behavior with their abusive partners. For both men and women, group counseling is the place to release their grief instead of dumping it on their friends or on their partner.

Couple And Individual Counseling

In addition to group counseling, I also recommend couple and individual counseling. One-on-one counseling is necessary for a couple of reasons: first, you can have your own personal program which is tailored for your personal needs. While ERMs are similar, they also have their differences. Many feel safer grieving alone than in a group.

Secondly, there needs to be accountability. Many times a husband will report in the group that everything is going well at home, and yet, if I ask the wife how things are going, she will tell me something different — that he is not taking his time-outs, and that he is lying about his abusive behavior. Likewise, there needs to be accountability in doing homework.

There is a lot more to recovery than just attending meetings. As we'll discover in later chapters:

- ERMs need to take time-outs.
- ERMs need to fill out anger journals.
- ERMs need to be good to themselves.
- ERMs need to monitor their thoughts.

These are matters in which ERMs need to be accountable to someone else. Accountability is much easier to monitor in couple and individual counseling than in a group setting.

How Long?

Finally, how long should counseling last? As long as it takes! I recommend a minimum of six months, but one to two years is better. One of the guys in the group once said (and everybody laughed when he said it), "I'm cured but I'm still here." What he meant was, he wasn't cured, he knows that he needs to come for a while, but he tries to convince others that he is cured. Many times he tries to talk himself out of coming back to the next session. That is why a partner's support is important. The more outside support you have, the better off you are. It takes time, awareness, and pain to recover.

In my own personal program, which lasted for three years, I progressed steadily through several phases. The first phase was the **learning phase**. I read all the books I could about abuse and I had that "ah-ha" experience. I began to see that it was my problem. This lasted about a month, initially, although I continue to review books to refresh my memory.

The next phase began when I started to attend group counseling. I call it the **behavior phase**. It broke my isolation. I admitted that I had a problem and the admission allowed further awareness. I began to monitor my thoughts and tried to control my abusive behavior and its escalation with positive self-talk. I was now aware of my thoughts and behavior, but still in denial of their underlying cause. It was at this level that I first thought I was "cured." Now I know that that was not so. The most painful part was yet to come.

The third phase I recognized was the **grief phase**. It was very painful and lasted approximately one and one-half years. I released a lot of anger at the source. I discovered while grieving that the source of all my anger was the abuse I had suffered in my childhood, physical and emotional. The pain was almost unbearable at times. I understand why many ERMs stop at this point, but it is the most crucial phase of recovery. It must be experienced to allow complete healing to begin. Otherwise, you will be taking "time outs" the rest of your life.

I proceeded to the **cognitive (or acceptance) phase**. I went to a specialist who did individual counseling in NLP (Neuro-Linguistic-Programming). She used a technique called RET (rapid eye therapy) plus another technique called anchoring. It removed negative thoughts and replaced them with positive ones. Also, with the help of another counselor, a cognitive therapist, I retrained myself to look for the good in everyone and everything and ceased being judgmental toward myself and others.

I began to feel love and acceptance for everyone. I call this final phase the **love phase**. It is a phase marked by an absence of denial, anger and addictions, grief, thinking disorders, and selfishness. It is a lifetime goal and requires constant awareness to keep from falling back into old habits.

I saw myself progressively moving through these phases, which represent the grief cycle. They are like layers of a sphere: in the center is love, then, proceeding outward, comes acceptance, then grief, then anger and addictions, and finally, denial. I call these layers the "Layers of Self-Deceit" (LSD Theory). To recover, I had to remove one layer at a time until the process was complete.

I broke the outer shell of denial by becoming teachable. Reading books (bibliotherapy) pushed me forward out of denial and into examining my life. I eliminated my anger and addictions by using behavioral therapy. This layer (the anger and addiction) was like a layer of insulation, numbing the grief that was below. It also numbed my ability to feel love and acceptance, allowing me only to "feel" anger, lust, and other addictions. The only way to get rid of the grief layer is to grieve it away, and Inner Child therapy is the best way to do that. Breaking through grief, I proceeded into the acceptance phase. There I dealt with the cognitive (thinking) issues of perfectionism, love, approval, and achievement. I needed to rethink my life and my "inner map" of reality.

The inner circle is love, the innocence with which I came to earth and had forgotten. I also call it the "Light" at the end of the tunnel. This Light draws me back to my innocence, illuminating the process of recovery, and helps me find power to strip away my imperfections, anger, and addictions. This power, I now know, is my Higher Power.

To The Partners Of ERMs: When Completed?

The best way to know when your partner has completed his therapy is to go by your feelings. If it doesn't feel right, it probably isn't. ERMs most likely to succeed are those with a good track record in at least one other area of self-improvement, i.e., he has stopped a bad habit, has educated himself, etc.

The Parable of the Sower from the Bible describes those who drop out of therapy. Four types of people are represented by the four types of soil receiving seeds: the seeds cast by the wayside are blown away. These drop out immediately (if they show up at all), they have no desire to change. The seeds cast upon stony ground have no roots and soon wither. There is no real commitment to change. The seeds cast upon thorny ground are those who quit when the going gets tough. They see their pain (the layer of grief), and the other prices to be paid for recovery (time and money), and decide that it isn't worth changing.

However, there are those tossed upon fertile soil. They overcome all the obstacles. The ground (hard, stony, thorny, or fertile), is in the ERM's mind and *the change must come from within themselves*. No one can be "forced" through recovery.

A New Beginning

Finally, where do you find a counselor? First, be aware that there are several types: MDs, PhDs, MSWs, MAs, etc. But no matter which letters the counselor carries, be certain that he/she has a high degree of experience in anger and abuse counseling.

Most important, go by your feelings. Leave the counselor if you feel uncomfortable. You want a counselor who instills trust, has empathy, and will take your hand and slowly lead you out of denial and into reality. There are many painful feelings that must be faced, but this must be directed in a caring manner. Inside every ERM is a frightened little boy, with tender feelings covered by grief, addictions and rage, and finally denial. They don't need further shaming but a firm resolve to change.

I never again want someone to look at me the way that counselor looked at me after Kate told her of the abuse, as if she was looking into a spittoon. Those were the same looks I received, while growing up, from my parents and others who taught me to act abusively in the first place. What I wanted was someone who saw my perfection on the inside and would be willing to help me remove the layers of imperfection that were covering it. I thank God for the treatment center I located and the book *Learning to Live Without Violence*.

~ 6 ~

"TIME OUT!"

STEP ONE: REAL AND PRACTICE TIME-OUTS

As Phil S. is arguing with his wife, he feels his chest begin to constrict. A faint pounding begins in his head. Phil knows these signs — he is ready to explode and become abusive. "I'm beginning to get angry. I need to take a time-out. I'll be back in thirty minutes." As quickly as he can, he moves toward the door and begins walking around the neighborhood. He begins talking to himself, "No reason to be upset. She is doing the best she can." In thirty minutes he returns in a calmer state of mind.

The first step toward stopping your abusive behavior is to learn how to take a time-out. A time-out is simply removing yourself from the presence of the person toward whom you feel anger. The steps I list below come from *Learning to Live Without Violence* (1989, pg 4-6) by Daniel Sonkin and Michael Durphy.

Before you can start your recovery, you need to stop the violence. The rest of the therapy for your recovery (the other eleven steps), helps in phase one of the three phases of violence (the build-up phase). Time-outs should be taken before phase two (the blow-up phase) is allowed to escalate. It is very important to learn how to walk away before violence begins. If I had known how to take a time-out while I still was married, I could have saved my former wife a lot of grief and pain.

There Are Four Steps To Taking A Time Out:
– The first is the "I" statement, "**I am…**" Be assertive. Take charge of your own life.

– Step two "…**beginning to get angry.**" Take control of yourself early, before the anger escalates into abusive behavior.

– Step three "…**I need to take a time-out.**" Another "I" statement. Continue to be in charge of your actions.

– Step four "…**I'll be back in thirty minutes.**" Leave and then come back in thirty minutes.

Practice Time-outs
The best way to learn how to take a real time-out is to take practice time-outs. First, go over with your partner exactly what you plan to do. Explain the why, when, where, and how of taking a time-out. If you don't have a partner, and you live by yourself, practice talking to a lamp or to the wall. The words are simply, "**I am not angry. I am taking a practice time-out. I'll be back in five minutes.**" Leave and take a walk for five minutes and then come back. Practice this several times, because when you need to take a real time-out it should already be a habit.

Remember The Following When Taking A Time-out:
– DO walk away quickly.

– DON'T stand there and argue anymore. Just leave. Walk out the door. Make sure you discuss this with your partner during your practice time-outs so she knows what is happening.

– The best activity to DO when taking a time-out is to take a brisk walk.

– DON'T drink, DON'T take drugs, DON'T go for a drive, and DON'T engage in any violent type of activity, such as chopping wood or practicing Karate, even if those are regular activities.

– DO practice positive self-talk while walking (see Chapter Eight). It helps lower your level of anger.

– DON'T continue your negative self-talk. If you do, you can have the same argument over and over in your mind. It was the negative thoughts that made it necessary for you to take a time-out in the first place.

– DO return thirty minutes later. This will establish trust.

– DON'T be longer. If you stay away beyond the thirty minutes, it will destroy all the trust you have built up by taking the time-out. When you return, if you are still angry, take another time-out.

– *DON'T stay in the relationship if the violence continues* after you have earnestly tried taking time-outs.

– I highly recommend that you DO allow a physical separation for a long enough period of time to allow healing of both parties. Relationships that have deteriorated this far need time and space to heal, if it is at all possible to heal.

Creative Time-outs

There are many places, however, where you can't take a time-out, such as when you are at work, or driving, or on the telephone. For situations such as these, there are several creative time-outs you can take. For example, when you are at work you can simply go to the bathroom. You can visit a co-worker, preferably a friend, with whom you can share your feelings.

In my contracting company, I developed a creative way to stop abuse. Anytime I would get angry with my workers or if I was being abusive and they saw it, they would earn $100. I only had to pay once. This was an extremely effective way for me to control my abusive behavior. I also realized that I couldn't stuff my feelings, so I began to practice being assertive. (See Chapter Ten.)

You can take creative time-outs when you are driving. For example, you can turn on the radio and allow yourself to slowly quiet down. Begin by tuning to a radio station that is playing very loud music that reflects the way you feel. Progressively change to more relaxing music until you are in a quieter mood. You can practice deep breathing. If the anger is severe, you can even pull off the road, count to ten, and say to yourself, "Everyone is doing the best they can." Especially be aware of your anger in the following situations: when you are behind bus drivers that are blocking your lane; when you are confronted by teen-agers who are driving recklessly; or, following slow drivers in the fast lane!

Another place to take a creative time-out is when you are on the telephone. You hang up the phone gracefully, simply saying, "I need to go now. Thank you." Don't slam down the receiver and don't answer if they call back. If at work, have your secretary or co-worker take your calls.

I remember once getting angry and slamming down the receiver while on a business call. The person I was talking with called back. I got angrier, yelled at him even more, and again hung up. When he called back the third time, I jumped into my car and went looking for him. This was *very* foolish and dangerous. I could have prevented it all if I had simply hung up the phone and refused to answer.

Practice Makes Perfect

I know time-outs are hard to do. During the escalation of an argument you want to stay and fight. The best way to prevent that is to take practice time-outs — at least three a week. I discussed the different levels of anger in Chapter One. They range in severity from being mildly annoyed (level one) to being extremely upset (level ten). I recommend that you start taking time-outs at level five and then begin to take them earlier and earlier on the scale.

I was a paratrooper while in the U.S. Army. We had two weeks of intensive training on the ground before we made the five air jumps that would qualify us for Airborne. I had practiced many times during those weeks doing static line jumps and PLFs (Parachute Landing Falls). My first two jumps from the plane were so automatic that I didn't realize what I was doing until I was on the ground.

Real time-outs will become just as automatic by taking practice time-outs. You will be walking away from the house before you even realize what you are doing. Or, gracefully hanging up the phone, or taking deep breaths while driving. It must become automatic. If you get into the habit of taking time-outs, you will stop behaving abusively.

Robert Robertson

~ 7 ~

"THAT'S NO EXCUSE"
STEP TWO: DRUG AND ALCOHOL ABUSE

George G. knows he is getting ready to blow up at his wife. Instead of taking a time-out, he drives to his favorite tavern. "What the hell — what's a few drinks?" The bar is mostly empty and he watches TV reruns. He thinks over and over about what happened and what he should have said. "Drinking," he says to himself, "allows my mind to think clearly and helps me relax." When he returns home, he has a violent fight with his wife which ends by her calling the police and having him arrested for a Class IV misdemeanor.

You've already learned to walk away from abusive situations using the time-out. You've also learned that reducing your stress (by walking during a time-out), and controlling your thoughts (by using positive self-talk) are essential for lowering your anger level. The first and most important step is stopping the abuse with time-outs.

As you've discovered by taking time-outs, stress and negative self-talk escalate internal anger (see Chapters Eight and Thirteen). Now, you must realize that drugs and alcohol also allow you to act abusively toward others much more easily. There are two reasons:

– First, drugs and alcohol lower your inhibitions, enabling you to do things that you wouldn't ordinarily do when sober. In chemistry classes I learned about energy and chemical reactions. The threshold of a chemical reaction is defined as the amount of energy required for a reaction to occur. Unless that much energy was present, you could mix all the chemicals together but there would be no reaction. A catalyst is anything that lowers that threshold and allows the reaction to occur with less energy present. That is exactly what drugs and alcohol do. They act as a catalyst and lower the threshold, making it easier for abuse to happen, when the "ingredients" of anger, stress, and negative self-talk are present.

– Another reason not to abuse drugs and alcohol is that it can later be used as an excuse for abusive behavior. You can say, "Well, I was drunk or I was on drugs and this is what happened." It is a poor excuse but allows rationalization. Using drugs or alcohol does not really cause abuse; instead it lowers the control of the rational part of your brain which regulates your actions. It shuts down that part (your "conscience") that differentiates between good and bad. At the same time, it opens up another part ("subconscious" hurts and pains) that allows all the rage that is inside to come out.

I quit drinking at the age of twenty-five but I was involved in several episodes of abuse before that age, while I was drinking. Once, I had a fight with a girlfriend and we separated for a time. During that separation, I went to her house one evening to have a "talk." I was so drunk that I put my fist through the glass part of her door, which allowed me to get inside at her. Frightened at what I had done, I drove home from her apartment and remember driving over a curb to avoid cars waiting for a red light.

I now realize that anytime you are drinking you can become abusive for a longer period of time and in a much more violent manner. I'm glad I quit drinking before my marriage to Kate. As bad as the abuse was during our marriage, it was never as bad as during the time I was drinking. Drugs and alcohol are a dangerous mixture for anyone with abusive behavior. Some people are "fun" to be around when they are drinking — ERMs, however, are "bad news!"

Addictions And Feelings

The purpose of all addictions is to mask your feelings of underlying pain by giving a temporary feeling of pleasure. In this sense, anger is also an addiction. It gives you a rush of power while you are acting out. Once I became very angry on a train trip and became abusive toward the conductor. I felt a tremendous rush of power inside of me and a great release of stress after being angry and abusive. Nevertheless, while I may have felt better at the time, my abusive behavior eventually destroyed all of the things I really wanted in life.

Stages Of Abuse

There are several stages leading to drug and alcohol abuse. First, you might be **experimenting** or trying it "just for fun." Then you become a **user**, with the drug becoming more and more important. Sooner or later, if you continue without treatment, you will turn into an **abuser**. Your life will revolve around getting high at any cost. You'll become so dependent on the drug that nothing will stop you from abusing it, including losing your job, family, health, possessions, or freedom. If you continue, the final stage is **early death**.

Again, I remind you never to fight with someone and then, instead of taking a time-out, go to a bar and get drunk. This is the *worst* thing you can do!

Recovery From Substance Abuse

The best treatment for drug and alcohol abuse is through NA or AA (Narcotics Anonymous or Alcoholics Anonymous), which use Twelve Step Programs. These groups can be found in almost all areas of the United States, charge no admission, are available days and evenings, and are highly effective. I recommend that you become involved with one of these groups first, while in anger recovery, and before you begin the "grief work" (See Chapter Fourteen).

John Bradshaw, in his book *Homecoming*, states that if you begin doing "grief work" and still have an active addiction, or that you've not had a year of recovery after that active addiction, you can easily slip back into that behavior. Also, you need to realize that residual effects induced by those chemicals can stay in your system for years. I've had clients in my group who have stated that they acted incoherently and had mood swings that involved anger, depression, grief and nervousness for several years after they stopped using drugs. This can be especially true if your entire life revolved around your addiction.

Again, drugs and alcohol are never excuses for abusive behavior, but when combined with anger, it is like throwing gasoline on a fire. If you are a substance abuser, you need to stop now. It will never be any easier than it is at this moment. It will only be more difficult and costly later. Stopping alcoholism in the later stages of ones' life is almost impossible — I know, since both of my grandfathers died alcoholics.

Relapses Are Normal

Don't be disappointed if you fail to stop the very first time. Set-backs are inevitable in recovery. The first time you fall you'll be surprised, the next time you may be angry, and if you have another relapse, you'll say to yourself, "Well, here I am again." But don't give up. Allow each set-back to serve as a starting point for future success.

I tried four times before I was able to finish college. It took three times for me to quit smoking permanently, and several dozen times to quit my other addictive habits. One by one I conquered them, but not without set-backs. Be gentle with yourself, accept yourself, and realize that if you really want to stop the habit, you will.

The Source Of Much Abuse

Drug and alcohol abuse is the source of much abusive behavior. I am an adult grandchild of alcoholic grandfathers. My parents were both adult children of alcoholics. Their irrational behavior toward me as a child is the source of all my pain and all my negative self-talk. My negative self-talk was an angry, two-sided conversation inside my head that was constantly arguing with everyone. The childhood pain and negative self-talk, when combined with current stress, was the source of all my abusive behavior.

In my contracting business one summer, because of injuries to two of my employees, I hired a group of men who were friends with each other to finish several contracts I was obligated to fulfill. While working with them, my reaction to their attitudes and behavior was to develop the most negative self-talk I've ever known in my life. I found out later that they were all alcoholics and drug addicts. It was only after I fired them that I realized what they were doing to my thinking. They stirred up "old tapes" of my parents' irrational behavior. I finally had to release that thinking (and them) before I had a relapse.

Beginning in infancy and continuing until I was a teenager, I suffered at my father's hands (and also my grandmother's after my mother died). I know all of that abuse can be traced back to the irrational behavior caused by my grandfathers' alcoholism. I believe that if alcohol had been eliminated in the early generations it would have eliminated abuse in later ones. The sins of the fathers are truly visited upon the heads of the children until the third and fourth generation.

It is up to you to break the chain.

Robert Robertson

~ 8 ~

"CONTROL MY THOUGHTS?"
STEP THREE: HEALTHY SELF-TALK

*For the past two weeks, Vince W. has been monitoring his thoughts.
"I can't believe it," he exclaims to the Tuesday evening men's anger
group. "My thoughts were angry all the time. I was constantly arguing with someone about something in my head. It really affected
my moods." Now, whenever Vince is angry, he changes his thinking
and practices deep breathing.*

Sometime into your recovery, you'll realize that your thoughts
can be your own worst enemy. Many of your "arguments" will
simply start in your own head. These thoughts will later be mani-
fested in abusive behavior towards another.

For example, when I was married, I did this quite often. While
visiting job sites in my contracting business, I would drive around
in my pickup arguing with my wife, Kate. The only problem was
— I was all alone in my truck. The argument was occurring totally
in my head. I would have a two-way conversation and she would
always be losing. I would grip the steering wheel so hard that,
when I sold it several years ago, I noticed that I had worn two spots
where my hands had gripped. When I arrived home in the evening,
I would greet her love with anger. Why not? After all, I had argued
with her all day. I had rehearsed it again and again. I'd taken both
sides. And she was always wrong.

What Is This?

This behavior has been called many things — inner conversations, the voices in your head. In the Twelve Steps program they call it "Stinking Thinking." I call it self-talk. I define self-talk as that conversation, which usually has two sides, that is going on inside your head. It can be good or bad, happy or sad, angry or calm. Mine, prior to recovery, was arguments with others. *It was such a natural thing for me to do that I was not aware of doing it, or of the damage it caused.*

The source of self-talk is your earliest socialization with significant others — your mother, your father, your guardian, your teachers, etc. Their voices, and the conversations you had with them, continue to be replayed inside of you. They can be critical or nurturing. For ERMs, they are always critical or worse. For many, there is a loss of identity. It is not "I do bad things" but instead it is "I am bad." Being reared in a dysfunctional family creates terrible inner voices. You have a lose/lose situation, no matter what you do.

Remember the story in the last chapter about the alcoholics working for me? I saw red nearly every day. It was pure hell. I continue to say that drugs and alcohol are the source of much negative self-talk, and pass on pain for many generations, polluting every tender mind with which they come into contact.

There is a special type of self-talk that you have to watch out for: trigger thoughts. They are quick, situational "buttons" that might be pressed when you are driving, when you're on the phone, or talking with children. These will be covered in more detail in the next chapter (which is about patterns and situations). These buttons can raise your anger level quickly, if you are under a lot of stress.

How Self-talk Affects Anger

In *Feeling Good, The New Mood Therapy* (1981), which is

about cognitive therapy, Dr. David Burns talks about self-talk and how it affects anger. Four steps are involved:

  – First, there is an external event — something we visualize, hear or feel happening. However, no meaning is attached until we start to "think" about it.

  – In the second step, what we think about the event causes the reaction, not the event itself. Our thoughts set the chemicals of the brain in motion.

  – Third, our thoughts cause us to have feelings, which give "meanings" to the thoughts we have. If our thinking is "bad" (or faulty), we will have negative feelings.

  – Lastly, we have a reaction, which is based on our feelings, which were based on our thoughts. Faulty thinking, then, causes faulty behavior. It is our perception of an event, not the event itself, that determines our feelings and subsequent actions.

Now, after recovery, I say to myself, "If I feel bad, my thinking is bad." I also know that no one "makes" me angry, but instead my thoughts cause these feelings.

Stress also plays a great part in abusive behavior (see Chapter Thirteen). Whenever you combine negative self-talk with stress, unless you know how to be assertive, be prepared for abusive behavior. This is why, when taking a time-out, it is important to use positive self-talk. Both walking and positive self-talk reduce stress and allow you to return, after a time-out, in a calmer frame of mind.

Four Steps To Follow To Change Your Self-Talk

  – First, **monitor your thoughts**. You can do this several ways. I used a timer, similar to the ones used in the kitchen. During work, while I drove around in my van or my truck, I set it to go off every fifteen minutes. I then wrote down my thoughts. I discovered that there were fifteen different categories of thoughts that I was thinking. You can do the same and lump them together in a way that is best suited for you.

– Second, **examine your thoughts**. *Feeling Good, The New Mood Therapy* presents an excellent procedure. Often thoughts contain one or more of the ten thinking disorders, such as thinking in black and white terms (everything is either good or bad), or over-generalization (if something happens once, it's always going to happen), or jumping to conclusions (reading other's minds, falsely predicting the future), etc.

– Third, **create a suitable self-talk phrase**. In other words, if you say, "These people are stupid," which is a form of labeling (identifying others by their behavior), you could simply change that to, "Everyone is doing the best they can." Put these affirmations on cards, or, better yet, make a self-talk audio tape, recorded in your own voice, with a two-way conversation. In other words, talk and answer yourself. My two favorite self-talk phrases are, "Everyone is doing the best they can," (this way I avoid judging myself and others) and secondly, "Keep calm, there is no reason to get upset."

– Finally, **learn to change your mood**. There are many effective methods you can use. Here are five I have used:

• One, memorize a song such as "Don't Worry, Be Happy." Singing songs always picks me up.

• Another is to take a "PMA (Positive Mental Attitude) Walk." When I need a lift, I walk around the neighborhood saying to myself, over and over again — like a "Howitzer Mantra," — "I love myself and I'm happy; I love myself and I'm happy." No matter how black a mood I am in, I can change that feeling and feel great.

• Third, listen to uplifting tapes and music (the kind without the heavy bass beat). I find "New Age" music the best.

• Fourth, I assembled a "PMA" book that was filled with

positive thoughts, affirmations, and beliefs. I look at it each morning before my period of meditation.

  • Fifth, change your body language. When I stand tall, I feel tall.

I want you to know that it really works. Self-talk, along with stress reduction, are two of the best ways to lower your anger level. I have had some very positive results.

One recent evening, while I was driving my car, a carload of teenagers cut in front of me. As I hit them with my high beams to let them know that I was a little unhappy with what they did, I got a "You're number one" sign from all of them. Ordinarily, I would have done something foolish. As it happened, I was in the midst of an intense discussion with a friend sitting beside me in the passenger seat. When I suddenly realized how angry I was becoming, I stopped reacting, gave myself a positive affirmation, laughed, lowered my high beams, and began driving slower. I wasn't stuffing my feelings away — it really works.

Positive self-talk works not only when you are angry, but it also works with feelings of low self-esteem, depression and other undesirable feelings. Of all the lessons I have learned about anger and abuse, this is probably the best method for getting immediate results. If you monitor your thoughts and change them, you will be astounded at the results.

Practice!

Demosthenes was a Greek senator and orator who lived between 384 and 322 B.C. To overcome a speech defect and shortness of breath, he practiced speaking with small pebbles in his mouth, on the beach before the roar of the ocean. I found that overcoming negative self-talk is just about as difficult. There are many obstacles on our mind, like the pebbles, and there are many obstacles outside of us, like the roar of the ocean. Many forces will try to return us to our former selves.

Changing your thinking is probably the greatest obstacle you will ever face. But it can also be the most rewarding when you overcome it.

My "tortured mind" was my own worst enemy. The "inner voices" which began in early childhood because of abusive caretakers continued to echo and caused damage later. Now, I have replaced the "attacker" with the "nurturer." I look for the good in both myself and others. My mind is now a pleasant companion.

~ 9 ~

"WATCH OUT — DANGER ZONE!!"
STEP FOUR: PATTERNS AND SITUATIONS

Scott and Betty M. always argue over finances, especially the checkbook. "It never fails — you don't record the checks you write," Betty exclaims. "Oh, yeah, well you never make the deposits with the money I give you," cries Scott. This ritual, fighting when they receive the bank statement, occurs each month. The thought of separate bank accounts had never occurred to them.

Bruce S. is talking about a fight he had with his son who is having problems at school. Bruce began to lecture his son and received hostile remarks in return. "Suddenly I realized that instead of anger, I was really feeling sadness about my own childhood. Somehow, his experiences triggered feelings inside of me that came from a similar experience. Instead of being angry, I listened and allowed myself to grieve over these feelings."

When I was a child, our family had a cabin in the country, which we visited each summer. The cabin was situated on a beautiful creek, approximately 50 feet across, with a dirt and gravel road running beside it. Every year, a road-grader leveled the road, removed the pot-holes, and spread new gravel. The road remained smooth all season, until the winter rains and traffic created new pot-holes and ruts.

Wouldn't it be nice if you could do the same thing with your mind — remove all the "ruts" of your faulty thinking, level it out, and then fill it with new thoughts? Every time you argue with someone, you increase the possibility of developing negative patterns of thinking and acting. If it is done over and over again, this behavior becomes like a rut in the road.

Kate and I had three steps in our pattern of arguing. First, she would do something — which could be anything which was not on my "list" of my desired behaviors for her. Second, I would come home, get mad, and blow up. Third, she'd point her finger at me and say, "You got mad." We would continue the pattern, defending ourselves and accusing each other, until it would escalate and I would become abusive. Over time the ruts got deeper until, like a car driving in the ruts of a road, our relationship bottomed out.

Buttons, Buttons, I Know Your Buttons

After a while, you are able to argue with someone just by giving them a look or making a snide remark. The pattern has developed so completely that you can go from an anger Level 5 to a Level 10 in a matter of seconds. These patterns then become "buttons," triggering angry reactions in moments that formerly took hours to develop.

NLP (Neuro-linguistic Programming) explains why this happens and shows how to change the pattern. The process is called anchoring. Think back to any sights and smells you had in your childhood. When you see or smell them again, as an adult, don't the strong feelings that were associated with them then come back? It is the same with looks, remarks, or other types of aggressive behavior. When you engage in any of those behaviors (a dirty look, a snide remark, etc.) toward your partner, those little cues "trigger" painful memories in the other person of old, bitter arguments. The solution is to change the pattern of the behavior between you and your partner. Anytime you become aware that an argument is about to ensue, find a new location in which to continue the discussion. Create a "neutral zone." For instance, you could go to a nice restaurant to discuss your problems instead of discussing them at home.

Other options might include swapping duties. Maybe you could do the housework and she could do the yardwork. The goal is to gain insight into your partner's activities and responsibilities. One day of doing housework and watching the kids will effectively change your desire for a "clean house at whatever cost."

Anytime you can change the pattern of the problem, you've solved half of the problem. The other half of the solution is to become aware of the looks and remarks that trigger responses in your partner, and *stop doing them*. Take a time-out if necessary.

Situations Of Abusive Behavior

Understanding situations is also important in controlling your abusive behavior. Patterns have to do with the method of your behavior, while situations have to do with the environment in which the behavior occurs.

When I was doing my anger journals (see Appendix), I noticed five situations in which abuse occurred or was provoked. The first was always with my wife (surprisingly not with my kids, because I swore I wouldn't abuse a child after the abuse I had suffered). Another was when I was driving the car, especially when I was behind slow drivers in the fast lane or rude drivers. The third situation was anytime I received a phone call from telephone solicitors or salespersons over the phone. A fourth situation was anytime I was working with employees or customers and there was a confrontation. Finally, anytime there was a confrontation that caught me off guard and for which I was not prepared.

To arrive at this awareness is the single best reason to constantly monitor your behavior with anger journals. Patterns and situations will reveal themselves and make the job of change easier. You will learn to become aware of a potentially abusive situation and change it before it develops. Most importantly, you can monitor your "trigger thoughts" and practice correct self-talk.

Situations Of Stress And Sadness

I discovered that there were other situations in my life that, instead of causing anger, caused stress or sadness. For example, after getting a haircut, I always felt bad and didn't know why. One day, I recalled from my childhood that my father gave me haircuts. Haircut time was one of the few times we would be alone together and he was always abusive to me. So getting my hair cut as an adult always brought back those feelings of getting a haircut from my dad. I broke the pattern of feeling bad by finding a barber who told jokes and by being assertive with him about getting my hair cut exactly as I wanted.

Another situation of feeling sadness was when I went to church. I remember my mom would have a fight with my dad because he didn't want us to go to church. Because my mother didn't drive, he drove us and he sometimes (when he wasn't visiting a "neighbor") waited in the car. He always had some snide remark to make about someone who he had seen while he was waiting.

Holidays depressed me, especially Christmas. One year, as a child, I got very sick after eating, and I thought it was the food. I now realize that it was the stress of all the different things that had happened over that particular holiday period. To overcome his guilt, after being abusive to me as a child, my father showered me with expensive toys. Sometime later (when I "misbehaved") I would be told how unworthy I was of such gifts. This phenomenon is called the "gift treatment." For example, parents will give children record albums and later break them; they will give sports equipment but never show up for the games, etc.

Another situation that upset me was school. I still get nervous when I walk down the halls and talk to the principal or the teachers. It reminds me of all the abuse I suffered at the hands of principals and teachers when I was growing up. The "permission" for them to be abusive towards me came from my parents. (Bobby "plays" too much in class; Bobby doesn't respect authority.)

The worst of all situations, however, was when I was eating dinner. As a child, that was the time our family had fights, and fights, and more fights. As I was the scapegoat, it always ended up directed towards me. I always had stomach pains and when I got older, I wanted to eat alone. Kate could never figure out why that was so. Dinner time to her was a time for sharing the day's activities and enjoyment of one another's company.

All the situations that caused stress and sadness for me as an adult were the result of enduring a childhood filled with abuse. Any similar situation in the present was anchored to those feelings from the past. Awareness (Anger Journals), grieving (Step Nine), forgiveness (Step Ten), and reframing my beliefs (Step Eleven) released most of the grief associated with those situations.

Special Situations

There are people in special circumstances where there is a lot of stress and yet there is nothing that can be done to change the environment. For example, you might be in the military service, or some form of confinement. These can be *very* stressful situations. I saw men explode in the barracks when I was in the service, especially during slack time. When they were not busy, it allowed them time to worry about their problems. The key is to stay occupied and not allow stress to build up (see Chapter Thirteen on stress reduction).

Other special situations that are accompanied by stress include periods of unemployment and debt, periods of recovery from a long-term illness, being confronted with a partner who has been unfaithful, or any similar apparent injustice.

Awareness/Letting Go

With all situations the key to solving the problem is awareness. By becoming aware of what happens to your behavior in certain situations, you can be prepared for it and begin practicing positive self-talk at once. Awareness comes from faithfully filling out Anger Journals *immediately* after each blow-up.

For ERMs, with their need to control, there is one final key: *letting go*. Let go of trying to control another's behavior and let go of allowing another's behavior to control you. I realized in all five of my dangerous situations, I couldn't control another's behavior but I could control myself. I could control myself by controlling my thoughts which controlled my feelings which ultimately controlled my behavior.

This is the greatest "control" you could ever exercise — controlling your thoughts and letting go of trying to control another's behavior.

~ 10 ~

"I THINK...I FEEL...
I WANT...I LISTEN"
STEP FIVE: COMMUNICATION TRAINING

Fred P. is having trouble at work with the boss. He is in charge of maintaining a warehouse and excess inventory is beginning to pile up. Ordinarily he has a blow up with his boss. This time he tries something new that he learned at his last group meeting. "Bill," he says, "there is no room left in the warehouse unless we start stacking things up. If something new arrives, it will have to sit outside. I feel frustrated at not being able to do anything about the situation. What do you suggest?" Fred's boss ponders the problem and arrives at a mutually satifying solution.

Sally J. is complaining to her husband about her shopping experiences of the day. "None of the dresses fit. Everything in my size was too big." Her husband, Brian, responded, "Well, try another size for crying out loud." He fails to really understand that she is bragging about losing weight. Instead of getting a compliment, she receives criticism.

Another behavior to learn is proper communication with others. Communication involves both listening to others and speaking correctly. Both are learned behaviors.

ERMs are poor communicators because they learned inappropriate behaviors as children. Not only don't they listen, but when they talk it is even worse. Many times they think they have said something that they actually never said. They will then argue forever, insisting that they said it. Or, they tend to be mind readers — that is, they project their own narrow interpretations onto what other people are saying, accepting it as reality, even if its completely off base. These cognitive problems with the ERM cause incorrect patterns of communication which heightens the chances of becoming abusive.

Three Incorrect Patterns

There are three types of communication patterns for ERMs. The first is passive. They stuff their feelings away and then never express themselves or say anything. They let stress build until they blow up. Another pattern is passive-aggressive communication. They give syrupy, sweet answers verbally, but give very hostile non-verbal answers (body language, voice quality, etc). Since most communication is non-verbal, their behavior is reminiscent of a Ninja warrior — they are standing in the dark waiting to stab you in the back. The third pattern of ERMs is to become aggressive and resort to one or more of the four types of abusive behavior.

Become Assertive

The solution to all these communication patterns is to change them and become assertive. Assertiveness means making "I" statements, just like you learn to do with time-outs. There are four steps to assertive communication, each step describing the process that is happening inside of you.

– First, make "I" statements when you physically sense something.

– "**I see…hear…smell**" — whatever caused your awareness of a problem.

– Second, give the cognitive part — "I **think**…" — and state your interpretation of the other person's behavior.

– The third "I" statement concerns your feelings — "I **feel**…" — and state your feelings about what you think they are doing.

– The fourth "I" statement is "I **want**…" You state the new behavior desired of your partner.

– A complete example could go like this: "I **see** you talking to another man. I **think** you are flirting with him. I **feel** jealous. I **wish** you wouldn't talk with him anymore."

Many times, by doing this, you find out that what is causing your angry feelings is, in reality, a cognitive problem. The feedback from the other person will "correct" what you really "saw" or what you are "thinking" or what you are "feeling" or what you are "wanting." They may change their behavior since they now know how it affects you. You'll also find that you release a lot of stress with assertive communication. Men in my anger groups find that, by expressing themselves (using "I" statements), they release most of the grief, pain, and anger that they're feeling.

Do's And Don'ts

Remember, when practicing assertive communication, there are four do's and don'ts:

– DO be patient and listen to your partner.

– DO express yourself fully.

– DO take a time-out, before becoming abusive.

– If necessary, DO get help or let go.

– DON'T push "I" statements down your partner's throat.

– DON'T stuff your feelings.

– DON'T let your feelings of anger escalate to the point of becoming abusive.

– Above all, you DON'T want to do this on your own if it *always turns into an argument*. Get someone to help you mediate your differences.

Other Ways To Improve

In addition to being assertive, there are specific situations where you may need to improve your communication skills. For example, you may have to learn how to say "no" — you find it very difficult to say no to a request, and later become angry at yourself or the other person. To correct this, learn to assert yourself and say, "Let me think this over and I will get back to you later." You can practice with salesmen, when someone calls you on the phone (telephone solicitors), or someone asks you to do something you don't want to do. It will allow you time to get in touch with your feelings and make a decision without feeling pressured.

Another opportunity for improvement is learning how to ask for what you want. ERMs do two things: they stuff their feelings and then later they explode. It is either black or white; there is no middle ground. Learn to ask for what you want. Practice with clerks, service people, and other "easy" situations before trying it out on your boss or spouse. Go through the four steps ("I see...I think...I feel...I want..."). Be firm in your resolve.

Lastly, ERMs are often guilty of expressing their feelings with the wrong words. In elementary school, as students, we would say "Can I" and the teacher would say "The correct word is 'may'." "Can" means the ability to do something; "may" means permission to do it. Similarly, you need to learn the difference between "can't" and "won't." Don't say "I can't" (meaning you are unable) when you really mean "I don't want to."

Take responsibility for your behavior and learn how to assert your feelings to others. You don't want to control others, but you don't want others to control you, either. When you stuff your true feelings away you are planting the seeds for negative self-talk. And ignoring your problems causes stress. Remember, negative self-talk and stress are the two causes of abusive behavior.

You Never Listen To Me

Probably more important than assertive communication, however, is learning how to listen. Kate's favorite line to me was, "You never listen to me." Of course I did. I listened to her. I "listened" to see if she was obeying me. What she really meant was that I wasn't listening to her feelings, I wasn't sensing her pain, nor was I understanding what she was talking about.

We are human "beings," not human "doings." We need to be sensitive to other people's feelings, and not expect "robot" behavior. Men and women are different in their desires and feelings, and each needs to be aware of those differences in the other. Women's main desires are to have affection, to talk with feelings, and to trust their partners with those feelings. Men, however, want sex, companionship, and recognition. Both men and women want all of the listed desires; however, men frequently emphasize one list and women another.

In many ways, these desires are very similar. Affection and sex belong together; companionship and talking with feelings are both excellent leisure activities, and recognition and trust are both necessary and acceptable feelings.

Yet, all of these desires are different. Many men wonder why their partner won't "make love" at night after they've been abusive to them all day. If they were affectionate all day to their partners, sex, the part men desire most, would be a natural thing at night. Women want to have sex with someone who loves and respects them, not with someone who uses sex as a tool of control or a third stage (make-up phase) tactic. Likewise, while men want companionship (a partner at sports events, parties, etc.), they should allow some of the time spent together to talk about feelings.

Finally, he wants to be recognized for his accomplishments and abilities and she wants to be able to trust him with her feelings. Both involve feelings, but different types of feelings. One involves a hierarchy dealing with relationships (recognition of his peers, a building up of self-worth), while the other deals with the quality of a relationship (sense of trust with her partner).

The best way to bridge the gap of desires between partners is to listen to each other. Communication models (visual representations of how communication works) usually have three parts: a sender, a message and a receiver. The message, research shows, is 93 per cent non-verbal. The actual words (what we say) account for only 7 per cent of what is heard. The other 93 per cent, the non-verbal, is what you really "hear." Therefore, correct (or active) "listening" involves both hearing the content, as well as paying attention to voice tone and body language.

Barriers To Listening

There are three barriers to active listening and all are inside of you. These barriers are your own thoughts, your own feelings, and your own senses.

– First, when someone is talking, you allow yourself to think ahead about what *you* are going to say when they finish and do not concentrate on what *they* are saying. Instead, simply listen to their words and repeat them to yourself.

– Likewise, many times your feelings get in the way — you interpret or judge or feel something about what others are saying. Again, eliminate judgments, and simply try to understand what they are saying. Take what they are saying at face value. Don't read anything into it.

– Third, you allow other sights or sounds to distract your attention from what is being said. The solution is to concentrate on the speaker and tune out the environment.

Two Paths

In their book, *Do I Have To Give Up Me To Be Loved By You?*

(1983), Drs. Jordan and Margaret Paul explain the two paths you can take in life. One is to self-protect and one is to learn. One says, "I'm correct and you need to change," the other, "What do I need to learn so that I can be a better person?" If you choose the path of self-protection, it becomes a barrier to listening. You blame other people. You don't want to hear what others have to say. Instead, you point your finger at them, insisting that you are right and they are wrong.

Only when you choose the path of learning do you accept responsibility for yourself and your behavior. Then you begin to listen and grow. There will be pain but you will find greater happiness at the end of the path. Both you and your partner's desires will be fulfilled, resulting in a life of greater joy. If you stay on the path of learning you will become a better listener.

Then your partner won't say to you what my wife said to me: "Bob, you never listen to me."

Robert Robertson

~ 11 ~

"I DON'T KNOW WHAT I FEEL"
STEP SIX — RECOGNIZING FEELINGS

Kelly A. was telling the group about his feelings. He is beginning to understand that there is something under the anger and rage. "Maybe I am sad or perhaps afraid. The other night my wife complained again about my job and having no money. This time, instead of blowing up and accusing her of spending too much, I just listened. I realized that my feelings were hurt because I was not able to provide for my family. It really cut me to the core."

If you have followed the program correctly through Step Five, you've made great progress at changing your **behavior**. You've learned how to take time-outs, to stop abusing drugs and alcohol, to practice positive self-talk, to be aware of patterns and situations, and to improve your communication skills. You are now ready for the next five steps, which have to do with your **feelings**. For ERMs, this can be difficult and scary.

As a child, I lost touch with my feelings. I buried them under layers of anger and addictions. Our family rules were "don't talk, don't trust, and, especially, don't feel." I knew my dad's feelings — anger and resentment toward me. My job seemed to be to try to satisfy him and to stay out of his way. Somewhere along the way, I learned to be in a "dissociated" state with my feelings. I could not associate with what was going on at the time. My feelings were "out of sync" with the events that were happening around me. When I did get around to feeling, it was always anger and rage, which I expressed by being abusive towards others.

ERMs can't "feel." Recall my "Layer of Self-Deception Theory" (better called "LSD Theory" because it really is a hallucination) which shows that love and acceptance are covered with grief, anger and addictions, and finally denial (Chapter Five). The grief layer, which is then covered with the anger and addiction layer, causes the inner feelings of love and acceptance to be hidden.

ERMs especially can't feel the pain they are causing and inflicting upon another person. The only things they can "feel" are anger, lust, resentment, judgment, and other addictions that numb the pain. Preoccupation with covering their pain also makes ERMs self-centered.

What Are You Really Feeling?

During abusive episodes, you've felt angry at people and situations. "How could you be so stupid," or, "This really stinks!" Many times, however, what you are really feeling, instead of anger, is something else. Anger is a secondary emotion. Primary emotions include grief, shame and fear. For example, instead of saying you are angry, what you really mean is that your feelings have been hurt. Or, you could be feeling guilty for your actions or feeling hurt about something somebody said to you.

Fear can be a very powerful feeling. Sometimes, not knowing what do to, you react with what is known as the "fight/flight" response. As a child, you took flight to avoid a fight, and later you learned to stand up for yourself. Now, instead of running away, you stay and fight. Strong physical signs (sweaty palms, flushed face, increase in heartbeat) accompany the "fight/flight" response, and can be recognized and controlled with practice.

A special type of fear is jealousy. ERMs can be *very* jealous. This jealousy is caused by many factors. For example, they probably have low self-esteem, which will be covered in Chapter Twelve; or, they create very negative self-talk, which is covered in Chapter Eight; or, more than likely, they have mistaken core values and beliefs, which we'll be getting to in Chapter Sixteen. In the extreme, ERMs, when jealous, proceed to very controlling behavior, and often act as though they were possessed by demons. These feelings of jealousy are usually unfounded or they become a self-fulfilling prophesy.

The key to recognizing your primary emotions (grief, shame and fear) is to be assertive and practice assertive communication, which you learned in the last chapter. If you talk the problem through, you will usually find that either your fears were unfounded or that they can be resolved by assertively working them out. You'll also become aware of the two other feelings besides fear (grief and shame) that are causing you to be upset.

ERMs feel bad feelings, but they don't allow themselves to feel good feelings. You need to be aware that there is an entire spectrum of feelings. Just be aware of good feelings and allow yourself to feel them — feelings such as joy, wonder, happiness, etc. Sometimes ERMs feel guilty if they want to have a good time. They need to learn how to be good to themselves (see Chapter Thirteen - Stress Reduction).

Getting In Touch With Your Feelings

There are three ways to get in touch with your feelings. One of the best ways is through the anger journals such as the one included in the Appendix. Anger journaling presents valuable information about what is going on inside of you. It helps you to recognize the patterns you've set up, hear the self-talk you are creating, and to become aware of the physical signs of anger *before* you explode. Physical signs include tightness in the chest, faster breathing, cold hands, and other bodily indicators. In my own experience, anger journaling showed me the five situations of which I needed to be aware; it showed me what my self-talk was doing to fuel my anger; and it showed me ways to avoid confrontation — I learned to get away whenever I felt flushed in the face.

Another way to get in touch with your feelings is through meditation. Become aware of your inner state. I found flotation tanks to be the best tool. A flotation tank is simply a closed container large enough for a person to lie down inside and is filled with warm water and salt. Once inside you are totally deprived of all distractions to your senses. In that deprived state, I became aware of physical feelings of which I was previously unaware — stiffness in my neck and shoulders, difficulty with breathing, and other physical discomforts. Then, I progressed to realizing my internal feelings — feelings of fear and anger and loneliness. I began to examine the reasons for each feeling and the thoughts and beliefs that caused them. I also learned that it is impossible to have stiffness in my neck and shoulders and have relaxing thoughts at the same time. I learned how to create relaxing thoughts, and so was able to get rid of the stiffness in my neck and shoulders, and my breathing became much easier.

The third way to get in touch with your feelings is through introspection. I did this by taking what I call my "PMA walks." I took brisk walks to clear my thinking. As I examined my thoughts and feelings, I noticed that I became angry when someone said something to me that "hooked" something inside. For example, if they said something critical of my behavior, it would bring up old childhood memories of criticism. I also remembered that I had fears of rejection, fears of abandonment, and other childhood hurts. These "hooks" go away during the grieving, forgiveness, and cognitive phases (Steps Nine, Ten, and Eleven). For now, you must simply be aware of them. As you get in touch with your feelings (and we'll go deeper and deeper into this area), you'll learn how to grieve over early "hooks" and get rid of them.

Becoming A Real Person

I realize now that feelings are more important to me than the rational, logical part of my brain that I valued so much before my recovery. I especially realize how important it is to practice correct thinking. I allow myself to experience joy, peace, prosperity, and love. Most importantly, I am still able to cope with conflicts and problems.

Not long ago, I had an interesting experience with someone who was attempting to fix the transmission of my car. I discovered that he was being dishonest about the claims he was making, saying I needed repairs immediately. I couldn't understand that logically, but since I was in touch with my feelings, I intuitively knew that what he was suggesting wasn't true. My feelings, I realize, are better than my logic at solving my problems. A second opinion on my transmission showed my intuition to be correct.

Each day I talk with my friends, share my feelings with them, and am very real with them. It is a great way to release stress and to help me become a genuine person. It allows my feelings to be expressed before they "dam" up and burst forth as anger.

Robert Robertson

~ 12 ~

"I AM...I CAN"

STEP SEVEN: BUILDING SELF-ACCEPTANCE
AND SELF-CONFIDENCE

Chris W. is the sharpest dresser in the group. He constantly talks about different women he has dated. After several sessions, we begin to realize that he is hiding behind a mask. In a moment of honesty, he painfully admits, "Yeah, I guess I am a lot of show and no go. I mean, I change jobs every six months, usually one step ahead of getting fired, and I'd love to have a permanent relationship. I guess I am living a lie."

Now that you are starting to connect with your feelings, it is time to examine the most important feeling that you have — self-esteem. ERMs, in general, have very low self-esteem. As children, along with the physical abuse, there was emotional abuse. "You are _____ (stupid, ugly, etc)."

Mine was, "It's Bobby's fault," — everything was my fault. I was the scapegoat of the family. I was the one that they tied all the sins to and kicked out the door. Somewhere along the way I bought into it. I became convinced that it was the truth. Of all the abuse I suffered, this was the worst. Because I totally accepted it, this became one of my core beliefs (see Chapter Sixteen). This core belief generated much of my negative self-talk.

Ingredients Of Self-esteem

Self-esteem consists of two parts. There is the acceptance part, that is, the "**I am**" — your feelings of self-worth, the feeling that you are O.K. There is also your self-confidence — the "**I can**" -- your abilities and knowledge, the perception of yourself as able to do or not do something. As a child you learned not only that "you can't" but that "you aren't" — you became the negative label. Not only was your behavior bad, you became "bad."

Types Of Self-Esteem

Psychologists have discovered two types of self-esteem. The first is **situational self-esteem**, that is, in certain situations you feel confident and in others you don't. The second type, which is more true with ERMs, is **characteristic self-esteem**, the "I am" type. You become the label. The key to raising your self-esteem is to change your thoughts and erase the self-critic, the inner tapes inside your head that seem to play over and over again. That inner critic is a combination of the voices of your parents and other authorities which have become embedded in your thinking. (For further reading on the subject, I recommend the book, *Self-Esteem*, by Matthew McKay).

Thoughts, Addictions And Self-Esteem

Remember that thoughts effect feelings, which in turn, effect behavior (Step Three — Self-talk). However, they have nothing to do with reality. "I feel (bad), therefore I am (bad)" is emotional reasoning and is false. Also, addictions serve to cover over the feelings of low self-esteem. Therefore, you must rid yourself of addictions before you can begin to raise self-esteem (Steps One through Five).

Seven Ways To Raise Your Self-esteem

Over the years I have acquired several effective techniques to raise self-esteem: the first, as stated above, is simply to **control your thoughts**. Control your thoughts in the same manner as you did with negative self-talk and anger. This time, instead of monitoring your thoughts whenever you are angry at someone else, examine them when you are angry at yourself, whenever your self-talk is destroying you. Use your timer, monitor your thoughts, examine the thinking disorder, and correct it with positive self-talk. By doing this you will achieve a new feeling of higher self-esteem.

Many times during the course of the day, I felt good and consequently thought I was good. Then, later in the day, I would feel bad and think I was bad. Could I have changed from being good to being bad all in the same day? Of course not. The only change was in my thoughts, which affected my feelings and behavior. I learned I had the power to control my "state of being" by controlling my internal dialogue.

The second way to build your self-esteem is to **give yourself little successes**. Make a list of easy things to do and whenever you do them, reward yourself. Brag on your behavior. This is called behavior modification and it is powerful. It works. But you must be consistent.

Third, **get a planner and use it faithfully**. Every time you accomplish something written in your planner, scratch it off, even if it is simply getting out of bed and fixing yourself breakfast. I love to scratch things off my planner, because that is the best way I know to reward myself.

Fourth, **don't ever set yourself up for failure**. This past year a friend of my exercise partner at my health club was going to start working out with us. His New Year's resolution was that this year he was going to work out five times a week. In previous years he had not worked out more than about once a month. He set himself up for failure. He came in once and never returned (worse than the previous year). A wiser choice would have been working out once or twice a week at a very easy pace. *Set realistic goals.*

Fifth, **nurture yourself and others**. Whatever you do, avoid being judgmental toward yourself or toward others. Learn to interrupt the critical voice inside you and turn it into a nurturing voice. Simply say to yourself, out loud if necessary, "I am tired of hearing these lies. It's not true and I won't believe it anymore." Then find ways to pay yourself verbal compliments and look for the good in others, too.

Sixth, **obey your conscience** -- don't do things you know to be wrong. Dishonesty, behaving abusively, and other types of incorrect behavior, all lower your self-esteem. Incongruity between beliefs and actions is guaranteed to cause guilt and erode your self-esteem.

Seventh, and most importantly, **obey the gentle urgings of your Higher Power**. Accept the grace that is offered you from God and surrender to it willingly (see Chapter Seventeen).

Loving Yourself And Others

ERMs desperately want to connect with others, but they either lack the feelings of worth — "I am," — or lack the skills to do so — "I can." Instead they act out with anger, addictions such as drugs, alcohol or sex, and other false or delusional ways of interacting with others. Raising your self-esteem, raising your "I am" and "I can" levels, will soften the frustrations which lead to stress and "acting out" toward others or "acting in" toward yourself. Raising your self-esteem brings you closer to becoming an authentic human being, an Emotionally Responsive Male vs an Emotionally Repressed Male.

~ 13 ~

"I'M GOOD TO MYSELF"
STEP EIGHT — STRESS REDUCTION

Eddie C. works two jobs to make ends meet. Any spare time he has he spends fixing up the house or working on his car. He came to the group only after his wife threatened to leave if he didn't get counseling. "I haven't got time to do this. Can't she see I am doing the best I can?" Closer examination reveals that Eddie doesn't exercise, has a poor diet, is a chronic smoker, and worries about practically everything.

I want you to imagine a shoe box filled with postage stamps, say, between ten and fifteen thousand of them, from every country in the world. What a job it would be to organize them! They would need to be separated into their different countries and then placed in a stamp book one at a time. Wouldn't it have been better to put them into the book one stamp at a time as they were acquired? If you continue to put off organizing them, soon the box will become so full that the bottom will fall out, scattering the stamps all over the place.

Stress is the same way. Like stamps in the box, it collects until there is no more room and something has to happen — the "bottom" falls out. It is better to solve your problems as you go, one "stamp" at a time.

Earlier in this book I compared ERMs to a pressure cooker without a valve that had been placed over a burner. The key is to put a release valve on the pressure cooker before it blows up. That "release valve" is, in addition to positive self-talk, stress reduction. Now that you have discovered your feelings (Step Six) and you have raised your self-esteem (Step Seven), it is time to get in touch with your physical feelings. Stress, along with negative self-talk, is the underlying cause of abusive behavior.

Causes And Sources Of Stress

One of the primary causes of stress is unrealistic expectations, either for yourself or others. Unrealistic expectations lead to frustration, which then leads to stress, which leads to acting abusively. The key to eliminating many abusive situations is to lower your expectations. Simply "let go" and relax. Surprisingly, you'll get more done and have better relationships with others.

There are many causes of stress:

– For example, you could have **physical stress** -- a weight problem, physical disabilities, or perhaps you are dissatisfied with your overall appearance. You may have a job that causes neck and eye strain each day and a drained feeling every evening after work.

– There could be **social stress** -- a lack of friends, a lack of things to do, or a lack of social skills.

– Perhaps you have **financial stress** -- lack of money, a low-paying job, bills piled up, or even being laid off work and having creditors at your door.

– But the worst stress of all is **emotional stress** -- induced by mental confusion and angry, raging voices inside your head. You are internally out of control so you try to control your externals and everyone with whom you come into contact.

Ways To Reduce Stress

One of the best ways to reduce stress is simply to do something good for yourself. ERMs, as a rule, neglect taking care of themselves. Many ERMs go to one of two extremes — they are workaholics, or just the opposite, they sit around and do nothing. Either way, they have a constant build-up of stress. I have found the following to be some of the best methods for being good to yourself and reducing stress:

– **Physical stress.** Take yourself out to dinner, buy a new wardrobe, or begin to exercise and get rid of the chemicals of stress that cause anger. Any aerobic exercise, such as running, swimming, or hiking, will rid your body of those chemicals that cause stress (check with a physician first *before* beginning any exercise program).

– **Social stress.** Join a club and make new friends. Call someone on the phone or make a date for lunch. Be "real" with people and they'll like you even more when they get to know you.

– **Financial stress.** Talk with your creditors instead of avoiding them. Arrange ways to pay off debts, if necessary. Live within a planned budget. Consumer credit counseling is free. Eliminate smoking and drinking, by getting help if necessary, and use the money saved for other needs.

– **Emotional stress.** I recommend relaxation and meditation for the relief of emotional stress. I have experimented with three methods:

• My favorite is progressive relaxation. To begin, sit comfortably in a chair and slowly "talk" to each part of your body and allow it to relax, starting with your head and ending with your feet. Progressive relaxation is very similar to self-hypnosis ("My hands are warm and heavy, etc.").

• Another way to relax is through biofeedback. Two types, thermal or muscular biofeedback, are excellent ways to teach your body how to relax. Biofeedback is simply giving an auditory or visual signal to your senses about how relaxed a particular part of your body is. The equipment can be elaborate or simple and is found at places such as health food stores or "new age" record stores.

• A third method that I find exceptional is a flotation tank (I talked about this earlier) — lying in a closed, isolated tank that is filled with warm salty water. It is impossible for the body to be tense and the mind to be relaxed at the same time.

– After achieving a relaxed state by using one of these three methods, I filled my mind with soothing and reassuring visualizations and positive affirmations ("I am loving and lovable").

– One of the best ways I've found for stress relief, however, is to do something out of character: play without guilt, learn to sing a song (if you are not used to singing, this could release a lot of stress), go to a playground and swing on the swings, or go to a library and read the joke books. These are some of the many ways you can rid yourself of stress. Be good to yourself — you deserve it.

Problem Solving

One of the things I have not yet discussed, and have intentionally avoided until now, is problem-solving. Many couples (mostly at the ERM's insistence) want to begin problem-solving immediately when they start counseling. This is a mistake — the "problems" are caused by the ERM being filled with unresolved grief of childhood.

I **strongly** suggest that you wait until you have finished all the steps up to this point, especially those having to do with time-outs, learning proper communication, and getting in touch with your feelings. Only after you have learned how to communicate with your partner and have gotten in touch with your feelings are you ready to problem solve. Otherwise, you'll be creating more problems than you solve.

I know of two ways to solve problems. First, complete these three steps: define the problem; list all the solutions; then implement the best solution.

For example, there was a little boy who came to his dad and said he needed to borrow some money. If his dad had thought that the money was the issue, he would have either given him the money or said no. But upon quizzing him carefully, he found out that the boy had a friend who was going to the store and he wanted to go, too. What he was really after was not money but the forming of a stronger friendship with the other boy. His dad suggested that he take the two of them to the drive-in for hamburgers. They readily agreed. By asking questions about the request (problem), looking for solutions, and then implementing the best solution, the problem was solved. But remember, they first had to communicate their real intentions.

A second way of problem-solving is simply "letting go." Some problems can't be solved easily, if at all. Letting go means caring about others but not trying to control them. It means caring about the welfare of a person but not doing for him or her what they should do for themselves. Letting go is realizing that you can't do everything for them. In that realization, you also let go of the stress it is causing you.

Five Rules For Arguing

Finally, if you are going to have an argument, play fair! There are five rules to follow:
- One, speak and then listen. Take turns.
- Two, no escalation or abuse.
- Three, stick to single issues.
- Four, learn how to compromise.
- Five, if all else fails, let go or take a time-out.

A Word Of Caution

There are three things that you DON'T want to do to relieve stress:
- DON'T fight it out or have a confrontation. It does not solve

anything. It may release your stress for awhile, but someone will always have to bear the brunt of that stress and will be worse off at the end of the argument.

– DON'T engage in any dangerous activity such as fast driving, especially after an argument. This endangers your life as well as others.

– DON'T continue "acting out" in a compulsive, addictive manner:

- DON'T have sex with another partner.
- DON'T go on an eating binge.
- DON'T drink or take drugs.

These activities, while appearing to relieve stress, are only temporary salves and often lead to greater problems.

There are healthy and unhealthy ways to reduce stress. Practice only those that are healthy and that reinforce strong self-worth. Being *good* to yourself is the key.

The Pain Is Yet To Come

When I finished this step, I thought I was finished with my recovery. I thought I had changed my behavior (especially my self-talk), gotten in touch with my feelings (by reducing my stress), and that my abusive behavior was behind me. There was no way for me to know that the next four steps — grieving, forgiveness, core beliefs, and surrendering to my Higher Power — would be the hardest steps to follow.

Real change begins and ends with these four steps. You become a new person who is totally connected with his deepest feelings, who has forgiven his childhood offenders, who has modified his core beliefs, and has returned to being a loving and lovable person (a childlike innocence). My recovery to this point (Step Eight) took nearly a year. Completing the recovery required another two years and a great deal of emotional pain and work. It is imperative that you don't quit at this stage. At the risk of sounding cliche-ish, the best is yet to come.

As we say in group, "The only way out is through!"

Robert Robertson

~ 14 ~

"SO THIS IS WHY I AM ANGRY!"
STEP NINE: GRIEVING FOR THE PAST

Today, I gather all my childhood pictures and look at each one. I hold them in my arms and cry. I emotionally embrace myself at each age. "I was a lovable little guy. Why was I abused?" I ask myself. I emotionally gathered each child and left home. From now on I was going to be their parent. For months now my massage therapist has been telling me about a new wrinkle I am getting between my eyes. I have been crying so hard that my face is becoming contorted. The pain is almost unbearable but I know I must continue until the tears are gone.

I remember a story that my dad told me of how he and my mom met. I didn't realize how significant it was until later. They were coming home from their first date and he said, "I'd invite you into the house, but I can't, because my dad's an alcoholic." My mom said, "I understand, mine is, too." Both of my parents were adult children of alcoholics. Both were raised in hostile, alcoholic environments. Neither of them was emotionally available to me my entire life.

I worshipped my dad for years, which is not uncommon for those who were abused, and I refused to criticize him. Many times I was angry with my friends who did. No one was allowed to criticize my dad! As a matter of fact, in a college sociology class I tried to put my family into the upper-middle class level, by making up things about my dad. Today I am not bound by blind loyalty to my family. I know now that the source of all my anger was the abuse I suffered in my childhood. Many of the masked feelings I had (hidden under anger and rage) were guilt, loneliness, sadness, and low self-esteem, caused by neglect, abuse, and finally, abandonment. I now realize that all of those feelings had their source in the alcoholism of my grandparents.

Why Grieve?

Many counselors proclaim that "we don't want to know why you are angry, we just want to help you change." I believe real change comes from grieving over "why" we're angry. I'm not suggesting it be used as an excuse to be abusive, but rather, as a source of pain for a starting point of recovery. *I take full responsibility for my behavior. Real change comes only from acceptance of responsibility and a willingness to deal with the pain first.*

Several years ago, one of my anger groups met with group leaders of an out-of-state program dealing with anger management. The two leaders of that program had been conducting group therapy for over eight years. The program consisted mainly of behavior modification and feeling work, but no grief or "Inner Child" therapy. One of the members of my group confronted one of the leaders of the other group. The leader blew up right in front of us. I could see the veins in his face begin to swell, his face turned red, and he started swearing. I said to myself, "Eight years in group and look what happened. What is the use of trying to change?"

The tools you've learned so far are to control your behavior and learn about your feelings, as they relate to anger. Grief work gets right to the source and eliminates the cause of anger. Do you remember the example of the glass of carbonated water (Part II)?

The bubbles represent anger. When the bubbles reach the top, they become abuse. Each step so far has gone deeper and deeper into dealing with anger management. Grieving (Step Nine) eliminates the "bubbles" of anger; forgiveness and changing core beliefs (Steps Ten and Eleven) get rid of the "bubble-maker."

A Time To Weep And A Time To Laugh

As a child, I never had time to grieve. When I was growing up I was always told, "I'll give you something to cry about," or I'd be called a "cry baby" if I cried after being punished. My proudest moment came when I stopped crying and fought back with my grandmother. I'll always remember that time. I grabbed both of her wrists to prevent her from hitting me. She had a terrified look in her eyes. I held on for dear life. I said, "You are never going to hit me again, you're never going to be abusive to me again." After that she was never physically abusive to me again. (I found out later that she had had a similar confrontation with her stepmother when she was a teenager.) So much was coming at me as a child, that I was out of touch with my feelings. The only feelings I knew were fear of my dad and my grandmother.

Connecting with my feelings required that I grieve away all the pain I had repressed since early childhood. Every tear I cried released anger and the deeper feelings of shame. Every tear now removes more hatred and rage, heals my wounds, and connects me with my "Inner Child." I know with a surety what the Scriptures mean in Ecclesiastes 7: 3-4: "Sorrow is better than laughter, for it is by the sadness of the countenance the heart is made better. The heart of the wise is in the house of mourning..."

In my opinion, the failure to take responsibility for your behavior, to repent and change, to grieve your loss, to forgive the behavior of others, and to form new beliefs, is the cause of almost all the problems of the world today. ERMs are unable or unwilling to do so.

They are stuck in the denial and anger phase of the grief cycle. Simply put, they refuse to be humble enough to surrender their pain by grieving. They continue to pass on that pain to others and blame others (individuals, classes of people, or even nations of people) for their (the ERMs) abusive behavior. The results are a world filled with violence, bigotry, and even warfare.

Stages Of Grief

The grieving process has several stages or steps that you must pass through:

– First is shock and denial. You deny the pain inside or discount it as being insignificant.

– The next step is to become angry. Sometimes you hope for a miracle. However, after this, most ERMs return to the denial phase. They sense the pain inside and choose not to deal with it.

– The third phase of the grief cycle is the actual grief itself. It is where the healing begins.

It took over a year and a half for me to get through this step. At first I had a very angry cry. The pain came in waves several times daily. I had rage mixed with tears. Memories of abuse flooded my mind. Then I went into deep crying. Memories of deep hurts surfaced. I would say (or my Inner Child would say), "Why, Daddy, why?" Finally the pain began to subside. I started crying a healing cry; at the end of each grief session, I began to feel relief and forgiveness.

– Eventually you arrive at the acceptance phase, accepting everything that happened. Acceptance doesn't mean you liked what happened, it simply means you have grieved the pain of what happened; thereby fully acknowledging its existence. You are then free to begin working on core issues (Step Eleven).

Dangers Of Grief Work

John Bradshaw, in his book, *Homecoming*, says you should do the original pain work or the grief work first, then learn new behaviors. However, he does warn about rage. For ERMs, I suggest doing the behavior and feelings work first (Step One through Eight) and then the grief work. Especially be certain that time-outs are occurring automatically and that other skills, such as positive self-talk and interpersonal communication, are well-developed. Calming the "rage within" is a tough process to go through.

Because of the extreme danger that might exist, I recommend that you have supervision as you go through this step. You can become very depressed, experience very low self-esteem, or have periods of uncontrollable rage. *Without guidance, you could harm yourself or others.*

Transition — "The Pit"

Now the transition begins. The old you (your false self) begins to dissolve and the new you (your real self) begins to emerge. The grief you feel at the loss of your old self, as well as the stored pain of childhood, can be overwhelming. After all, up until now, they have been your constant, if painful, companions.

But, as I finished the grief cycle, I stepped forth on the other side of the pain as a new person, a cleansed person. I experienced true inner peace for the first time in my life. There was no more "acting out." My public self and private self were the same. I was renewed and enriched. I felt great!

The transition stage between the old and new me was terrible. I became one of the "walking wounded." I was on very unsteady ground. The transition stage is the "pit" — a hole from which you cannot seem to escape. You are unsure of yourself, you don't know how to act, and others don't know how to react to you. This is why many men stop at this point. You let go completely of one pillar (the old you) and grope around in the dark until you grasp the new pillar (the new you, the real you). It is scary to feel as if you are without an identity. But like the group leaders I mentioned earlier, you can work for eight years on your behavior and it will be useless at times without doing grief work.

What Do You Grieve Over?

The purpose of grieving for the past is to grieve over the abuse you suffered, whether it be emotional abuse, physical abuse, or sexual abuse. Get closure with these stored memories and they will affect you no longer. As you cry, these memories will flood into your mind, even events that are now totally blocked from your awareness. Even when blocked, the feelings are still there to contaminate your behavior. The blow-up stage of abuse is simply a reliving of those events combined with current stress and negative self-talk.

Memories that I blocked were triggered by looking at pictures of myself, especially those taken when I was a year old and seven years old. I can now actually remember the episode when I was a year old and my dad was trying to teach me to walk and how abusive he was to me. I remember my older sister trying to help me. I remember sitting on the floor and crying. I remember the feeling of terror! I remember clearly the episode when I was seven years old and getting my picture taken on Easter. I've looked at that picture many times and cried.

You need not only grieve over the abuse you suffered but also the neglect — the lack of skills that you should have learned as a child, the feelings you stuffed away, and the love you didn't receive. Perhaps your parents didn't have any time to be with you or you didn't have the opportunity to learn the skills you wanted and needed to learn.

I have grieved over the neglect in my childhood, which still surfaces occasionally in my relationships with others. I have also grieved over feeling abandoned by my mom when she died. I have grieved over my dad's rejection of me as he withdrew into his own hellish addictions. And I have grieved over the treatment I received at the hands of my grandmother while she was my guardian. My consequent abusive behavior toward my former wife, and others in my life, has extracted a great price from me — the loss of my family and many wasted years — and over that I have also grieved deeply.

More than anything you need to grieve for your thinking disorders. Changing your thought patterns will be one of the toughest challenges you will ever undertake. (More on that in Step Eleven.) You need to learn how to constantly monitor your thoughts so you can shut down that inner critic that is being judgmental and critical.

I was surprised to discover how much grief was being hidden by the addiction of "stinking thinking."

Several Methods Of Grieving:

– Write a letter to someone who caused you pain. You don't need to mail it. In fact, you can burn it when you're done. Or, you can write in a journal. Write all your thoughts and feelings down on paper. Energy that has been held onto for years can be released.

– Another way to grieve is through group and individual counseling. If you feel safe, go ahead and share your feelings with others. This is the principle behind such groups as ACOA (Adult Children of Alcoholics).

– Another way is to talk to a chair (Gestalt), or take a bataka and beat on the cushion of a chair. Pretend your abuser is in the chair and express your grief, rage, or other feelings to him or her. Some of the men in my group say this is a great way to release anger.

– Another way is to read *Homecoming* by Bradshaw, and reclaim your Inner Child step-by-step.

–The best method I found to relieve childhood pain is by crying. By crying I was able to get to the deep levels of pain. A friend, who had been through recovery, gave me a tape by Samuel Barber called Adagio. As I listened to that tape (I was taking a long drive), the haunting strains of the violin music brought tears to my eyes. As I repeatedly listened to the tape I "taught" myself how to cry and connect with the past. The music was a good trigger for getting me to grieve, and the incidents of abuse automatically came to mind as I went deeper and deeper into my subconscious.

Remember my description of an ERM: an emotionally disabled man who is normal in other ways. Grieving integrates the emotions with all your other attributes (physical/intellectual/spiritual) and allows you to play "catch-up," turning you into an adult in all ways. This catch-up is the most difficult phase of recovery — it is easy to return to the abuse cycle prematurely before the pain is gone. You must continue until there are no more tears —the only way out of the pain of rage, shame, and loneliness is through it.

When Do You Know The Grieving Is Finished?

When you can grieve for another, when you can feel the pain you have caused someone else, and when memories of abuse are less painful, then you know this phase is nearly completed. Ridding yourself of that burden will allow you to be less self-centered and more other-centered. After you stop acting out with abusive behavior, you need to grieve over the loss of other addictions (sex, critical thinking, etc.) that covered the pain below. Each addiction is covering pain.

You need to grieve over your anger and your rage stored from childhood. You need to grieve over your judgmental and critical thinking. You need to grieve over the loss of not acting out sexually, if this has been a problem. All serve to cover pain and must be eliminated in order to feel the pain below. I recommend that you grieve over them *one at a time* and repeat the cycle until you are abuse- and addiction-free.

I thought I was going to cry forever. It was the lowest moment of my life — I was totally alone and depressed. But it was at the end of this grief that I discovered the Light at the end of the tunnel. I even discovered the purpose of my life and the importance of going through this painful experience.

Grief was a barrier, like a layer of insulation, that separated me from feeling love and acceptance for others. Instead, I only allowed myself to feel anger and lust — addictions I used to cover the pain — and remained in denial of my behavior and true identity. It was only after going through the grief level that I began to feel forgiveness instead of anger, acceptance instead of judgment, and love instead of lust. Only then could I feel another's pain, and I lost desire to inflict pain, through anger or lust, upon them.

But It Wasn't That Bad At My House

I believe many people were not allowed to express anger because of religion or because of loyalty to their family and strict family rules. Many men in my group came from very strict homes, homes without love that outwardly appeared to be very religious. They were not allowed to express anger and they still have a fear of breaking the commandment, "Honor thy father and thy mother." Many minimize abuse as discipline. Many were neglected and taught that their feelings didn't matter.

I believe that anger and grief are absolutely necessary parts of the healing process. I've now forgiven my caretakers and know that they did the best they could, but before I could learn to love them, I had to be angry at them and grieve over my stored pain. The healing came after the shouting and crying were over.

Don't continue to say everything was (and is) okay. Don't continue to deny. You cannot say good-bye until you have said hello.

Robert Robertson

~ 15 ~

"I'M SORRY"
STEP TEN: FORGIVENESS

Darren and Shelly C. have been coming to couple counseling for approximately three months. Darren has made great strides at changing his behavior but is frustrated by Shelly's reaction. She says, "I am afraid to trust him with my feelings. He has hurt me too much in the past." "Yeah, well," he responds, "for the last month it has been payback time. No matter what I do or how good I am, she finds something to yell at me about. So, how am I supposed to forgive her if she won't forgive me?" "Forgiveness," I say to Darren, "is not conditional upon the other's behavior. However, it is necessary, even required, for your own healing."*

By using the last four steps (feelings, self-esteem, stress reduction, and grieving), you've begun to connect with your own feelings. However, you really can't solve your anger problem permanently until you begin to connect with another's feelings. Step Ten (Forgiveness) begins the process. You will become less self-centered (with your own pain) and more "other-centered" (with the feelings of others).

* Authors Note: This chapter is directed solely to ERMs and their need to forgive. I advise anyone with an abusive partner NOT to accept the abuser's behavior. Forgiveness and acquiesence are clearly two different things. Though you may forgive your partner, to continue to give in to the abuse is dangerous and you should remove yourself from it as soon as possible. Submitting to the abuse in the name of forgiveness helps no one, including the abuser. You do not need to apologize for his behavior. It is his responsibility to seek professional guidance.

Prior to these steps, I couldn't feel another's pain and I occasionally believed other people were in some way responsible for my anger. As I connected with my feelings and those of others, I realized that I had created a great tragedy by destroying my marriage.

Forgive To Be Forgiven

Most religions teach that we must forgive others if we want forgiveness. Why is this so? Is there a law upon which this principle works? I believe there is. Forgiveness requires humility. When we begin to humble ourselves we become teachable and flexible rather than self-protective and defensive. Also, as we become forgiving toward others, we tend to more easily forgive ourselves. ERMs, in general, are very hard on themselves.

Practicing forgiveness is sound advice if we remember our objective, which is to change our behavior, not to get even and punish others. Good people are good because they were loved and nurtured in childhood by their parents and others and now, through positive self-talk, they love and nurture themselves. Judging and criticizing doesn't change a person's behavior.

Think about it. Did the harsh, abusive behavior, the judgmental treatment that you received as a child make you a better person? Did it make you want to do better or did it make you want to be angry and abusive? My upbringing caused me to be anything but "good." The same is still true today. Remember the counselor in Chapter Five and the "spittoon" look she gave me? I didn't feel at all like changing my behavior for her — or toward her. In fact, just the opposite was true. Is the objective to get better or to get even?

Ways To Practice Forgiveness

There are three important parts to forgiveness. First, forgive others for their behavior. Begin by making a list of those persons, whether real or imagined, whom you feel are responsible for your abusive behavior. Then write them a letter. Letter writing is best because it gives you a chance to organize your thoughts. It also releases energy while you write and there is no chance for escalation. You don't even need to mail this letter. If you feel your forgiveness will not be accepted, burn it or throw it away and forget about it. After writing the letter, simply let go and forget the incident.

Don't expect your letter of forgiveness to be met with acceptance immediately. This is especially true in two cases: the partner you abused, or your caregivers who caused you to be abusive. With your partner, an interesting phenomenon begins when you stop the abuse. She still needs time and opportunity to vent her anger. Men in my groups complain that, after they stop their abusive behavior and their partners feel "safe," the partner lets go with all her anger. This will diminish with time and shows the value of having a woman's group in which your partner can release her pain. She's always felt angry but she has never felt safe enough to express her feelings. Many times victims of abuse hold on to that anger for years and are unwilling to forgive their abuser and certainly do not feel they have done anything that requires forgiveness. As an ex-abuser, there is really nothing you can do to force a person to accept your forgiveness.

Rarely do caregivers who were abusive admit their faults (my dad thought he was perfect until the day he died). In fact, if confronted with any accusations of mistreatment, they often become defensive or hostile. In such cases, it is better to write the letter and then burn it. The purpose of forgiveness here is to help **you** heal. You may, if you feel safe, bring it to your group or counselor.

Second, ask for forgiveness for your behavior from those with whom you have been abusive. Write a letter of accountabililty. All twelve-step programs suggest taking responsibility for your actions and letting those involved know of your sorrow. Be sincere about what you are saying, admit your abusive behavior, and ask for forgiveness.

I strongly suggest that you do not include any specific incidents that could be used against you in court. Be careful not to allow this letter to be used against you by a still angry partner. Also, never admit to things that would involve another person without their consent. For instance, if you had had an affair with someone you wouldn't want to mention a name.

Don't expect the other person to readily forgive you. Years of abuse can take years to forgive. Just accept their feelings and don't become angry at them or yourself.

Third, forgive yourself. Be good to yourself. Nurture yourself through changes of behavior. Be kind to yourself when you have relapses. Remember: that harsh, abusive voice in your head is why you are now abusive. Stop abusing yourself first. It doesn't help you get better, anyway.

Dos And Don'ts

– DO be sincere. Practice looking for good in others and you will find it in yourself.

– DO believe that this process works even though it takes time. Forgiveness is a process and not an event.

– DO listen to comments that other people make back to you. They may be painful, but those comments can serve as a great teacher.

– DO think of yourself as a diamond in the rough. It is going to take lots of time and lots of chipping away to remove all the rough edges. But underneath lies a polished jewel!

– DON'T expect others to ask for your forgiveness or to apologize to you. You must forgive unconditionally; it is not meant to solicit a response from others.

– DON'T expect others to notice the change in your behavior, at least not at first. Not only will they not apologize but often they may have what is called a "frozen evaluation" of you: you're bad, you're abusive, you're whatever the negative label is that they have assigned to you, and always will be.

– DON'T apologize for someone else's "stupid behavior." In other words, you shouldn't use this letter to further criticize your partner or be abusive.

– DON'T use the letter as an act to manipulate someone. Letter writing should only be done when you are well along in recovery and are sincere about everything you feel, and are not trying to keep someone in an abusive relationship.

My Own Apology

Not long ago, I had two opportunities to briefly experience the hell that I gave Kate for twelve years. One occurred while I was talking on the phone with an acquaintance. She was upset over something I had said the previous evening. As we talked, her feelings escalated and she became angrier and angrier. She'd been married twice and her ex-husbands were alcoholics. She felt she needed to use a sledgehammer to get my attention when perhaps a tap on the shoulder would have sufficed. Because I cared for her, I felt sick at my stomach with pain at what was happening. Again, I believe alcoholism is the cause of much negative self-talk.

The second time I witnessed abuse was when I was talking to a couple in my office. The husband was one of the men in my first anger group. He became extremely abusive to his wife right in my presence. I watched her reaction to his words and abusive behavior. She was in so much pain! For the first time in my life I was able to see that every word he said to her was like a punch thrown into her stomach. I truly sympathized with her.

After these two episodes, I began to understand the pain I had inflicted upon Kate and started to feel genuine remorse for my behavior. I wrote this letter to her, and also to everyone:

> Dear Kate,
>
> I'm sorry for all the pain and abuse you suffered at my hands, for the abuse the children witnessed, and for the break-up of our marriage. I accept responsibilty for this. I also forgive you for anything you have done to me, and hope and pray that someday you can accept my forgiveness and likewise forgive me.
>
> Sincerely, Bob

~ 16 ~

"I BELIEVE"

STEP ELEVEN — CORE BELIEFS

Eric S. appeared calm and serene. "It has been a long road, but the worst is behind me. I still can not believe the way I used to think. I now realize that I did not like myself nor anyone else. Women... boy, the way I believed real men treated women. Well..."

Each stage of recovery removes one layer of learned imperfections and uncovers another (hence the name "Layers of Self-Deception"). Each layer removed brings us closer to our perfection. The first layer removed was the "shell" of denial, followed by the "insulator" of anger and addictions, and onto the "smoke" of stored pain. When you have finally grieved away all the pain of the memories of childhood, underneath you'll find the last layer. These are your core beliefs, beliefs that began in infancy and were formulated in early childhood. Beliefs that form the foundation of all your thoughts, feelings, and behaviors.

After my grief was gone, I discovered that my beliefs were very negative. I call this last layer the "fire" — the fiery thoughts that drive the entire system. This fire creates the smoke of grief, a need for an insulator of anger and addictions, and a shell of denial to present a false self to others (and to yourself).

One night I seemed to be able to "see" this layer — a representation of all my beliefs. This representation appeared as the topography of a city at night with all the lights out. There seemed to be four clusters of buildings which represented my four beliefs: my belief in a Higher Power (perfection), my belief in myself (love), my belief about other people (approval), and my purpose in life (achievement). The darkness represented how negative these beliefs were. The "smoke" of grief had prevented me from "seeing" them.

I realized that I needed to modify many of my beliefs. Otherwise, grief would be recreated from these beliefs, creating a need for anger and addictions to insulate me from new painful feelings. Also, I realized that my father had colored all four areas of my beliefs.

Four Primary Areas

What are these core beliefs? They are the literally hundreds or thousands of thoughts and attitudes that were formed in early childhood. They can be grouped into four areas.

The first was my belief in God and truth — all the beliefs that I had about Diety, perfection, and the purpose of life. Next were my beliefs about myself — my abilities, my self-worth, and my personality. Third, my beliefs toward others — relationships (especially with females), authority figures, and cultural differences. Finally, my purpose in life or my goals. I examined each of these and worked on changing them. To examine them required several days of monitoring my thoughts to uncover these beliefs.

For example, concerning my belief in God or my Higher Power, I discovered I had been guilty of seeking perfection and having black and white thinking. I was either the best or the worst, good or bad, or happy or miserable. I realized that my father had been demanding, critical, unnurturing, and condemning of me. I had imagined that my God was the same. Changing these beliefs brought great joy into my life. I changed by having "faith," one small "seed" of faith at a time, until it grew to "knowledge."

I became loving toward myself and knew that I was loved. I realized that my growth happens through making mistakes and then correcting them. I believed that there was always help available when I asked (through prayer). I began to see my Higher Power, not as someone who was critical, but as someone who was nurturing. I came to know God as a loving Father and felt safe to surrender to His will.

The next area of core beliefs that I examined concerned myself. My dysfunctional upbringing caused me to think that I needed sources outside myself to feel whole. I sometimes felt that I needed others in order to have an identity. I identified myself by my relationships with my friends and associates or with my partner.

To correct this core belief I needed to learn the art of self-love. I needed to realize that I was okay by myself and I needed to nurture myself by my thoughts and actions. I decided to stop dating and to get out of relationships entirely for a while. I began to realize that I could function independently and be whole on my own. I began to believe in myself and my abilities to relate to others in a positive way. I now know that people think of me as I think of myself. I must love myself first to be loved by others or to truly love them.

The third area of core beliefs centered on my thoughts about others. My dysfunctional childhood taught me to believe that I needed approval from others, even though many times I didn't care for them. Perhaps my motivation was to stop their criticism of me or maybe I was seeking their approval to stroke my own damaged ego.

To change required that I become proactive and not reactive, acting on my own desires and not reacting to others. If I wanted approval, I got it from myself or from my Higher Power. I stopped fearing authority and examined each of my prejudiced feelings. I began to look for the good in others and became less critical of them and their behavior. I practiced serving others and began to feel true love for them.

I especially formed new beliefs about women, their roles, and my behavior toward them. I learned the proper way to treat women both in and out of relationships. I stopped lusting after their "outer costumes" and began looking at their "inner beauty." I began thinking and acting in terms of friendship and equality.

Finally, I examined my beliefs about my purpose in life and my goals. My dysfunctional upbringing and current thinking said that I didn't matter or that I needed to be "perfect" to matter. Even though I had progressed far with my career, my appearance, my education, and other personal goals, it was never enough.

I realized that to correct this I needed to measure myself with a different yardstick — a yardstick that said where I was, where I had been, and where I was going — a yardstick, not compared to perfection, but compared to my own abilities and achievements.

All four of these areas had been colored by my father. All four of my core beliefs had been wrong. But I was unable to see them until I had removed the outer layers, until I had broken out of denial (the shell), until I had eliminated my abusive behavior and addictions (the insulator), and until I had grieved away all the pain (the smoke) that was covering this layer (the fire). Only then could I examine my core beliefs and only then could I begin to change them.

Changing Core Beliefs

After discovering what your core beliefs are (by monitoring your thoughts, writing them down, and grouping them together), there are two ways to change them. One of the most important things to do is to stop the inner critic, that voice inside your head that desires perfection and is constantly critical of yourself and others. I discovered that this voice, instead of making me reach toward perfection, is in reality the cause of pain and anger and other addictive behaviors. I chose not to listen to that voice again. Many times I would say, "I am not going to listen to you!" I created a new, nurturing voice. I said, "I love and accept myself unconditionally." With others I did the same thing. I would say, "Everybody is doing the best they can and is blameless for their behavior." I began to look for the good in myself and others. In other words, I replaced each negative thought with a positive one.

Second, I restructured my entire core belief system using NLP or Neuro-Linguistic Programming. I went to a practioner who developed a technique called Rapid Eye Therapy. Using the same process as my brain does at night when I am dreaming (REM Sleep), I was able to access old stored memories (which caused pain and addictive behaviors) and program in new thoughts (for behaviors that I wanted). Also, with another NLP method called "anchoring," I was able to replace the bad thoughts and bad feelings that I had with good ones.

To continue this process (I feel it should be done for a lifetime), I constantly monitor my thoughts, feelings, and behaviors to discover their underlying core belief. If I am thinking, feeling, or behaving a certain way, I examine the core belief that is causing those thoughts, feelings and actions. Many times a single belief needs to be separated into two beliefs — it's okay to "hate" a behavior but still "love" the person, instead of "hating" a person for a behavior you find distasteful or unacceptable.

I need to point out that changing your core beliefs is a very, very difficult process. You can only realize what those beliefs are after you've stopped the addictive behavior that is covering the pain below. Stopping the addiction allows you to feel and grieve that pain. The pain, like a layer of smoke, is covering your beliefs. Until you remove the insulator (anger and addictions), and smoke (grief), you won't be able to "see" your core beliefs.

You must constantly be on guard against negative thinking. Changing negative thoughts to positive thoughts is a life-long process of altering your core beliefs by the process I have described. It happens through inner choice, not outer influence — it is something for which you must take responsibility, not something others will do for you.

A Repentance Process

I believe that corrected core beliefs lead us home to our Heavenly Family and to grace. The word "repentance," which is translated from Greek, means "a change of mind, fresh views about God, about ourselves, and about others." Changing our core beliefs is truly a repentance process.

After having been in recovery for almost three years, I had stopped being abusive. I had also stopped grieving for the past. I was in the process of restructuring all of my core beliefs. The next step was to start looking for the positive and stop dwelling on the negative behaviors of myself or others. I needed to be a light to others and not stand in judgment. I was now ready for the final step, which is surrendering to my Higher Power and practicing unconditional love. Underneath the layer of "fire," I found the "pearl."

~ 17 ~

"I SURRENDER"
STEP TWELVE — YOUR HIGHER POWER

Marvin R. smiles as he relates his experience. "God has made a difference. I never would have believed it. I am going to church, I am reading the Bible and I am saying prayers. Wow, it is unreal. My life has really changed since I entrusted myself to His care." When he first walked into my office, Marv terrified me. That is saying a lot because I thought I had seen everything come through these doors. He appeared to be gazing ten feet beyond me as he talked. He was a former Marine and martial arts enthusiast. At the beginning, Marv spoke of going to a bridge and shooting people. He was filled with rage and hatred! Now his face was filled with serenity and love of people and life. He had done his work.

As I stated in Chapter Five, my road to recovery started when I humbled myself and began to surrender to God. I had fasted and prayed for an entire weekend and I received my answer the next week when I attended my son's gymnastics meet. Since that time, I've felt God's hand guiding me through all the phases of recovery.

The final step, and an appropriate ending to "recovery" and the beginning of "discovery" is to totally surrender your will to God. All twelve-step programs center on surrendering to a Higher Power — whatever you believe that power to be. The void left by ridding yourself of anger and addictions must be filled, and grace is the power that accomplishes that need.

Before finishing Step Eleven, whenever I examined my thoughts and beliefs about my Heavenly Father, I felt God to be like my earthly father — judgmental, punishing, and unloving toward me, yet favoring everyone else. I now realize that is not so. I look to Him for guidance and blessings in my life. I only have to examine the past and what it has shown me to know that many times I have been blessed. I have faith in a God that is loving and perfect. I believe that He wants me to succeed. The injustice I received in life (injustice I blamed upon Him), I discovered came from ill-informed and unskilled people.

Filling The Gap With Grace

As I humbled myself and looked inward, I saw my true reality and personality. I saw a large gap in my life between the skills I had learned from childhood until that time and the skills I needed to cope successfully, especially in my relationships with others. If I wanted to have that gap filled it had to be filled by grace. To receive grace requires asking for it by going through these four steps:

– First, you must have faith. You must believe in a Higher Power and understand that He is not like your earthly father, but is a loving God who desires your happiness.

– The second step is to have humility and surrender your will to your Higher Power. This is accomplished through prayer and meditation. Prayer is the act of allowing your will to reflect the will of God.

– Third, have remorse for your actions and change your behavior by changing your mind. Eliminate any residual anger and addictions, and not only practice forgiveness for acts you have done to yourself and others, but experience it within yourself as a completed process. Affirm that you will remain surrendered to that which you know to be right and in accord with what you now perceive as truth.

– Fourth, by following these steps faithfully, you will experience God's gift of grace.

In his book, *Life After Life*, (1975) Raymond Moody, in talking about near-death experiences (NDEs) states that he believes there are two purposes to life. One is to love (specifically unconditional love, which is not dependent upon another's actions) and the other is to obtain knowledge (especially to learn how to love). Feelings of love we have for ourself and others come through grace — "We love because He first loves us."

The opposite of love is selfishness and self-centeredness. Grace, which is the source of all love, comes from surrendering selfishness. Grace is a divine gift of help or strength which enables us to reach more of our unlimited potential after we have exhausted our own means.

Become As A Little Child

The rage we've felt all along, as ERMs, was from our wounded Inner Child. His needs never have been met. Instead he was abused, neglected and abandoned. His needs are still unfulfilled and he will continue to contaminate our behavior until those needs are met. One of the ways to fill our Inner Child's needs is through our Higher Power.

ERMs, like many others, are co-dependent. They need to cling to another person in order to feel whole. We were created that way. Only by being filled with grace from our Higher Power can we overcome co-dependence. "Love never faileth." Without grace, we would inevitably replace one addiction with another.

My Higher Power was truly the Light at the end of the tunnel. I know that He answered my prayer and illuminated the path before me. As long as I was humble and remained on the path to learn, my needs were provided. With Step Twelve, I became less selfish, self-seeking and self-centered. I stopped thinking of "me" all the time and started thinking of "we." Ironically, it was only after becoming interested in others that I found more joy in life. In losing myself, I found myself. This was the "pearl," my real and eternal self.

A New Beginning

There were many steps in my healing from abusive behavior. I have identified my problem, I have changed my behavior, I have gotten in touch with my feelings, I have grieved in behalf of my Inner Child, I have re-examined and changed my core beliefs, and now have surrendered my will to the will of my Higher Power. On occasion, a new distress comes into my life or old distresses come to the surface. I still need a process to handle that on a day-to-day basis.

The solution is to go through these steps (based upon the grieving cycle and my twelve steps), only at a much faster rate. At this stage of recovery, the process takes from several minutes to several hours maximum:

– At first, I break out of shock and denial and examine what has happened to me.

– I then allow myself to become angry over what happened, yet I know that I must manage my anger and not become abusive.

– Next, I grieve away whatever pain is present. Talking with a friend, or crying if necessary, helps immensely.

– I continue by practicing forgiveness and examining the core belief underneath. I realize that the incorrect belief is almost always the source of my pain.

– Finally, I surrender to God.

By going through these steps I am able to process any grief, shame or anger that comes to me.

Now, when I realize a problem is affecting me, I cycle through these steps. I don't allow my problems to build up. I will not let my feelings "dam" up like they did before, only to have the dam crack, crumble, and fall — which is the "other" cycle (abusive behavior). Instead, the flow is steady and pleasant, just like my new life. I return again and again to the "pearl" of love, breaking the "shell" of denial, eliminating the "insulators" of anger and addiction, grieving the "smoke" of unresolved pain, and quenching the "fire" of incorrect core beliefs. Each time I return, by overcoming the opposition, I become someone greater than the time before.

Having exhausted all my own resources, I can say truly that I owe my entire recovery to the grace of God.

Robert Robertson

PART III

Contexts Of Abusive Relationships

Freud called love and work the two pillars of adult identity. These, unfortunately, are also the two main vehicles of abusive behavior. I have divided love into two parts — love shared with wives or girlfriends, and love shared with children (Chapters Eighteen and Nineteen). Abuse in the workplace is covered in Chapter Twenty.

Robert Robertson

~ 18 ~

"YOU ALWAYS HURT THE ONE YOU LOVE"
(Abuse in Relationships)

Donna S. calls me requesting a session alone. She is considering leaving her husband after eleven years of marriage. She wants to get information about her husband's problem in order to make the right decision. "The final straw," she says, "is when he farted in bed after making love and then laughed about it. He is always putting me down. Why does he do this to me? Will he ever change?" This is the question all partners of ERMs always ask. "Will he ever change?"

ERMs don't have relationships, they take hostages. Almost immediately after the start of a relationship, the cycle of abusive behavior begins. First there is emotional abuse, then severe emotional abuse, until, if allowed enough time, there is physical or even sexual abuse. Patterns develop and buttons are continually pushed. Some partners recognize the signs and get out early; others stay to the bitter end.

Five Stages Of A Relationship

There are generally five stages in an abusive relationship. First, there is the **intact relationship**. At the beginning the relationship seems to be loving and caring, but the ERM is being manipulative and can be a great pleaser. Next, after several cycles of abuse, comes **emotional pain**. The partner of the ERM tries hard to please or understand him but cannot. Third, after more and more emotional pain, there is an **emotional separation**. Eventually the ERM's partner begins to give up and stops loving and trusting him. She no longer feels safe sharing her feelings with him. Perhaps she still hopes for a miracle. At this point she is still in denial of the real problem. Her self-esteem has been nearly destroyed by his continual abuse.

The fourth stage of the relationship is a **physical separation**. The separation can be temporary or permanent. It is usually triggered after a certain event — severe abuse, escalation from emotional to physical abuse, or abuse that involves others, such as their children.

If you are the partner of an ERM, this is the ideal time to encourage him into counseling. Don't be manipulated by third stage tactics (the make-up/honeymoon phase) that he uses to keep you around. The majority of men need to be compelled to start treatment.

It may be necessary to physically separate if there is severe emotional or physical abuse. This is a time for both of you to heal and face hard decisions.

The fifth stage is either to get a **divorce or attempt a reconciliation**. The choice should be made after weighing all the pros and cons. Go by your feelings. Ask yourself, "Is he going to counseling, is he changing?" ERMs most likely to change are ones that have demonstrated success in improving other areas of their lives, such as stopping any bad habit, continual job advancement, etc.

Watch out! This can be a very dangerous time if you decide to permanently separate. Severe battering and even death can occur when a partner confronts her abuser and insists he stop controlling her.

The Treatment

For ERMs, I recommend that you *allow* a separation (if the spouse desires) especially if there is severe emotional or physical abuse taking place. Begin attending group counseling and learning how to take time-outs, practice positive self-talk, get help to avoid drugs and alcohol, and learn proper communications skills. This phase of counseling lasts about six months.

Next, begin individual and couple counseling. Work on deeper issues, such as unresolved childhood grief and core beliefs. This should also last for about six months. Counseling is expensive but well worth the investment. It is impossible to heal alone, and, from my own experience, the price of counseling is much cheaper than the alternative: a divorce and its related expenses.

For the partners of ERMs I recommend a separation and, if necessary, a safe place to live and a restraining order if the abuse is severe. You need a time and a place to grieve. Group counseling is an ideal place. I also recommend family counseling if children are involved and/or if you desire to stay in the relationship. Individual counseling is needed to understand your co-dependency and reasons why you enabled him to abuse and control you. You may be able to reconcile if you feel it can work out; otherwise, separate permanently. This is something that should be decided with your counselor.

For both of you, be aware that this is a time to look out for "paybacks." Many times partners feel that the ERM is now "safe" and it is time for her to repay him for the abuse he did to her. This is normal and short-lived, but be aware of the phenomenon. Be aware, also, that this is a time of increased stress and tension. Let the counselor mediate any problems that confront the two of you. Work on your own problems and don't try to "fix" your partner. Both the ERM and his partner should attend their meetings and do their assignments to get well. If the ERM continues to be abusive, the partner should report that to the counselor.

Abuse counseling usually follows one of two formats. The first is the traditional approach which focuses upon stopping the abuse (simple behavior modification) In my view, this is not enough. To completely overcome abusive behavior requires greater changes such as changing beliefs about women. In addition to changing core beliefs, I believe it is necessary to include Inner Child (grief) work and spiritual therapy.

New Relationships

If you decide during separation to discontinue the relationship and begin a new relationship with someone else, please allow time. Both of you need time *before* rushing into another intimate relationship — time to heal wounds and change behaviors and beliefs. Healing while alone is the best way. Get in touch with your own needs and issues.

When you start over, be honest with your new partner. It doesn't have to happen on a first date, but before you get serious, talk about the past. Take time to get to know your partner. Make sure he/she fulfills your checklist of wants and needs. It is recommended you get counseling *before* you develop a permanent relationship. Counseling can uncover any potential problems and allow them to be solved or reveal the undesirability of a permanent relationship at that particular time.

Three Choices

There are only three choices available to handle abusive behavior in relationships:

– First, you can compel an ERM into counseling and hope he continues until he has changed. This is a process and not an event.

– Second, you can leave him.

– Third, you can stay and continue in the abuse. Abusive behavior, left untreated, will escalate over time, become more frequent (the cycle shortens), and become more dangerous.

– There is no fourth choice. There is no spontaneous remission. It is important to remember that during the third phase of abuse, ERMs can be extremely convincing that they have changed and will not continue to be abusive.

Without treatment, their words are simply meaningless and empty promises.

Robert Robertson

~ 19 ~

"DADDY, WHY ARE YOU ANGRY?"
(Abusiveness Toward Children)

By now, Sandra J. was accustomed to her husband's behavior. He blew up at her over a "mistake" and left, slamming the door. She had learned to emotionally separate herself from him to protect her feelings. However, this time something new occurred. Her five-year-old daughter, Stacy, came into the room where Sandra was standing. Stacy had heard the argument between her parents. Stacy heard how she was criticized for her messy room. Stacy heard all of the name-calling. With a look of lost innocence in her eyes, she said, "Mommy, why do daddies hate their children and their mommies?"

Even though I am now an adult, I have an Inner Child (the emotional and innocent personality inside of me). I'm traveling in today's body, but carrying yesterday's baggage. I'm dressed in today's clothes, but I am wearing yesterday's underwear. My freed Inner Child today is my constant companion. For years I ignored him, but now he is my best friend. Whenever "we" take walks together he likes to pretend he is a basketball star. He'll dribble the ball beside me, jump high into the air, and slamdunk a basket. Like the cartoon character, Calvin, in the newspaper comic strip

"Calvin and Hobbes," he has quite an imagination. Sometimes he is sad and wants to be held while he cries. Other times he is tired of being serious and he just wants to play. I can feel him being rambunctious when I am reading a book or any other "boring" activity.

Before he became my friend, he was very angry. My rage came when he acted out — when this three-year-old inside of me took charge of my six-foot, one hundred and seventy-five pound body and began to inflict rage and punishment on those around me.

A Training Ground For Abuse

Childhood is a training ground for ERMs and their mates. If your family was dysfunctional and abusive, you learned at least three things:

– The first thing you learned is that it is okay to be abusive — it is okay to give and take abuse. The belief about roles of parents and husband-wife relationships were solidified in childhood. Abuse was "the way" to settle arguments.

– Second, you were taught that feelings didn't matter — you were punished or at least ignored for expressing anger, pain, or grief.

– Third, you were taught how to be in denial — your family was to present an ideal appearance to the outside world. The rules of the family were: don't talk, don't feel, and don't trust.

My childhood punishment caused me to act out angrily later in life. I am not sure what results my parents expected by harshly punishing me, but I am sure they didn't get the results they desired (or perhaps, by making me the scapegoat, they did). Abuse made me do anything but want to behave later in life. I was proud of my stoic nature and learned to blame everyone else for my anger, just like my parents did. I got more than angry; I got even, too.

There Are Many Reasons That Children Are Abused:

– At the top of the list is their need for attention. Attention takes time, either from you or from your spouse. Kids need time to play; they need time to learn, and time to be shown affection. This inborn need for time and attention can make you angry because they are taking your spouse away from you or cutting into "your" time.

– Another reason children are abused is because they are expensive to raise. They need clothes, food, health and school expenses, and money for leisure activities. It can add up to financial stress.

– Also, children have excessive amounts of energy and are often noisy and messy. Rearing children is a time of repetitive, boring tasks.

– Finally, there are dangers in raising children. There is the continual possibility of accidents and they seem to get into trouble constantly, especially if they are seeking or craving attention from unresponsive parents or other important adults.

All these factors combined — their need for attention, the expense, the noise, the energy, the repetitive tasks, and the dangers — can add up to a lot of stress. This stress, which they probably don't know how to handle, combined with negative self-talk, can cause parents to become abusive. ERMs are already on "overload" with the stress they carry internally (unresolved childhood grief). Any additional, external stress is likely to trigger abusive behavior, perpetrated against the source of that stress.

There Are Four Types Of Abusive Behavior Toward Children:

– First, there is **emotional abuse**, usually in the form of name-calling (labeling), looks that can destroy confidence, and abandonment or desertion, or threats thereof. Severe emotional abuse in childhood becomes the "self-talk" in adulthood. Those names, looks, and fears stay with children forever.

– There is also **pet and property abuse** -- the abuser kicks the child's dog or cat, slams his fist into a wall, or throws things. This, while meant to elicit obedience, terrifies children. A woman of my acquaintance suffered a great tragedy in her childhood at the hands of her father. Because she had misbehaved, her father took her out to their barn, pulled out a handgun, and shot her pet horse. That event is marked indelibly on her memory forever.

– The next type of abuse is **physical abuse**. Physical abuse includes not only hitting, but grabbing, pulling hair, or twisting an arm or finger. Emotional abuse filled me with negative self-talk, but physical abuse filled me with rage. My only memories of my dad seem to be the times when he whipped me with a belt, or as he gave me those terrible looks, or when he called me names. The rest of the time he either ignored me or showered me with gifts to salve his own pain, after being abusive to me.

– The fourth type of abuse is **sexual abuse**. Sexual abuse in-cludes *any* inappropriate touching or fondling, as well as types of sexual name-calling (***Don't ever*** call this type of behavior ***love***!). Fortunately, I was never abused in this manner, but I feel certain that sexual abuse must be the most damaging type of abuse that can be inflicted upon a child. I am acquainted with several women who were molested as children. They have spent years in therapy and have paid a severe emotional price for the abuse they suffered. This can be just as abusive to men. Statistics reveal that one in three girls and one in six boys are sexually abused.

Options For Abusive Behavior

There are much better options for training and disciplining children than through the use of abusive behavior (called "corporal punishment" by those who still insist on using the rod). If you desire to have loving and well-behaved children, here are four things to consider:

– First, if you truly love your children, the best way to demonstrate that love is to love their mother. Acts of love and kindness to her will show your children the correct pattern of behavior toward others and assure them that they are safe and loved. Ironically, I was not abusive with my children during my marriage. I resolved in childhood that I would never treat my children abusively. Unfortunately, I was abusive to my wife, Kate. I now realize that I had initially trained my children to expect abuse in marriage. I've spent a lot of time since then talking with them and I am sure that they understand that this is not okay. It is never too late to retrain a child, but it would have been better had the abuse never happened.

– Second, allow your children to express their feelings openly and know for certain they can trust you with those feelings. Let them know that it is okay to argue at times, it is okay to express feelings, and it is okay to talk about anything without fear of some kind of reprisal. Give your children hugs, praise, and kindness. *listen* to them. Teach them correct principles (which form their core beliefs) about God, themselves, others, and their abilities with others. One of the greatest gifts you can give your child is a healthy self-esteem.

If you don't show your love or allow feelings to be talked about, your children will express them in other ways. Back in high school, those who I respected most were those who were close to their parents. The students who were really popular were ones whose parents loved them and allowed them to talk about anything. Strict, yet unloving homes, those where feelings were never expressed, produced promiscuous behavior.

– Third, spend time with your children. Plan it or it won't

happen. Events such as daily talks, weekly planning meetings, and periodic vacations are ideal. Teaching, talking, and events all take time. Spending time with your children shows them that you love them. Time together is always better than the "gift treatment" where one minute you are buying toys and the next you are criticizing them for their unworthiness.

– The fourth option, in place of abuse, is discipline. You must set up rules to be followed, then allow the discipline to be the natural consequence of their inappropriate behavior. Allow your children to set up the rules with you and agree upon the discipline if they are not followed. There is a big difference between discipline and punishment. Discipline teaches children the correct way to behave, whereas punishment reinforces the wrong behavior. Discipline takes time and shows you care, whereas punishment is short-lived and shows you don't!

Love Never Faileth

For the best results, be loving and lovable. I have learned many lessons in life, but I only learned to love from those people who were loving. Those whom I have loved best are those who loved me and wanted the best for me, not the ones who were the "I'll teach you" types. What I learned from the latter, I had to unlearn later in life.

To be loving first requires that you complete your own recovery. Consider the idea I learned while on a recent flight. Prior to takeoff, the flight attendant instructed everyone in the proper way to put on their oxygen mask. She said, "If you have children with you, first put on your mask and then help your children put on theirs." You are not being selfish by working on your own problems, for you cannot teach anyone something you do not already know.

~ 20 ~

"WATCH OUT FOR
(MR. SMITH) TODAY!"
(Abuse in the Workplace)

Shawn S., a client for approximately three months, reported that he was fired this week from his job. He initially came for counseling because of problems with his girlfriend and the resultant separation. He was beginning to understand that problems at home could affect his work. At our next session, he reported that he was able to convince his boss to give him one more chance by being placed on probation. "The boss says I am impossible to work with. Before, I would blame everyone else; now I listen."

The Bureau of National Affairs reported in 1990 that abusive bosses cost U.S. companies $5 billion annually in lost revenues and health care costs. The study showed that one in four is running his office in the same abusive way that he was treated by his parents as he was growing up.

In my opinion this is really just the tip of the iceberg. There are many abusers in the workplace — bosses, co-workers, customers, etc. Much of the stress caused by this abuse is stuffed away and taken home to partners and children. Like ripples on the lake when a rock is dropped in, it seems to affect everyone.

Abusive Situations

The men in my group counseling sessions say that next to the family, the second biggest source of stress and grief is their job. I have identified at least five abusive situations in the work place:

– The first is abusive supervisors. They often behave like little Hitlers. They may call you names, give you unrealistic deadlines, or tell you to do outrageous tasks. They can be very unpleasant to work for; or, they can be passive-aggressive and use subtle methods to drive you crazy, if you so allow.

– Co-workers can also be abusive. Like dropping ink in a glass of water, they tend to set the mood for the whole office. Whenever they are around, everyone feels uncomfortable. I've been in both situations — worked for a jerk boss and worked with fellow employees who were unbearable. That is why, over twelve years ago, I started my own business. I've never regretted that decision.

– Third, if you are a supervisor, you may have employees under you who can cause problems with the rest of the workers or with customers. This is something that you, as their supervisor, must deal with quickly or face special problems and even legal problems. It is especially true in matters of sexual harrassment, which is really a form of sexual abuse. When my employees talk, I listen.

–A fourth situation involves customers who make special demands, who are discourteous, or are simply a pain in the neck. It can be bad enough if you are the boss, but it can be terrible if you are an employee and they are on "favored" status with the business owners. If you have an unsympathetic boss and are constantly stuffing your feelings, this abuse is probably being unloaded on your family after work. Most of the men in my group say it's one of their biggest sources of stress.

– Finally, the job itself may be stressful, or the type of work you are doing subjects you to abuse. I am sure that people who write traffic or parking tickets are constantly in stressful and abusive situations. Air traffic controllers and ambulance crews face tremendous amounts of stress related directly to their jobs. Filling sales quotas month after month can take its toll. It is completely understandable why almost all jobs are called "work!"

Three Solutions

In all five of these abusive situations, the key to solving them is learning to deal with difficult people. I've discovered three strategies that deal effectively with abusive people:

– An interesting one comes from NLP (Neuro-linguistic Programming). It is called pacing. Simply reflect the feelings and mannerisms of people who are being abusive to you, without being abusive in return. For example, if someone says "I'm tired of this," join in and say, "Yeah, I don't blame you. I'm tired of it, too." Mimic their posture and expression. Once you've established a rapport with people, you are able to influence them in a positive way and elicit the behavior you desire.

– Second, don't enable abusers to continue being abusive. Practice being assertive and use "I" statements. Talk to supervisors about co-workers and customers who are abusive. Continue until you get results, whatever it takes. Be firm. But, if all else fails, let go of those feelings and, if necessary, seek employment elsewhere. Remember, in large companies there is such a turnover in personnel that you will probably have a new boss every six months. Some will be great and others will be jerks.

– Finally, if you feel you are being abused, you may need to learn how to take the person seriously but not personally. Abuse is wrong, ***but it is always the abuser's fault***. The odds are that they don't feel any personal animosity toward you. When they treat you with abuse, it is always because they just don't know how to handle situations differently. Instead of your anger, what they really could use is your understanding and/or pity.

Avoid them as much as possible and don't be abusive in return.

A Final Note To Supervisors

As a supervisor, there are three choices you have with someone who is abusive who works for you. One, you can continue letting them be abusive (I guarantee they won't change on their own). Two, you can dismiss that person (but be careful to avoid a wrongful discharge lawsuit). However, if you really value them, and your other employees, you'll insist that they get counseling. You are in a position to insure that they do something about their abusive behavior. You are not only helping them, but you are helping yourself. If they do something illegal to your other employees or your customers, you are liable for their behavior. In this litigation-happy world, the proper precaution is to firmly suggest that they get counseling before trouble occurs.

People today are demanding an abuse-free workplace. Free of sexual harrassment, free of abusive supervisors, and free of unneeded stresses to contaminate them and their families.

Employers and business owners, aware of this new attitude, can perform a great service by insuring their "human resources" are treated with respect and dignity.

POSTSCRIPT

To My Brothers In Anger

I hope that reading this book has helped you to recognize your problem and let you know that the problem lies within you and not other people. I hope it convinces you to change. I wish this book had been available to me years ago. For many of you, however, I know that parts of this book have made you angry or you are denying them. It is unfortunate if you feel that way. My intention has not been to make you angry but to help you.

I still say that you have only two choices. First, you can continue in the denial. You'll find the abuse will continue to escalate and joy will eventually disappear from your life. I watched my dad remain in denial and he was bitter until the very end. Sadly, most abusers choose this path. However, you can choose recovery. It is painful at first, but extremely fulfilling when it is over.

If you decide to change, be prepared to devote a lot of time to the process. At least two years. You'll know you have finished recovery when you can talk to anyone about your abusive behavior, when you are filled with love and trust for others, and when you are able to express your feelings in such a way that you are assertive and not abusive. Above all, you will know you are finished when you can feel the pain you have inflicted upon others and you accept personal responsibility for all of your actions. Then you are no longer an ERM.

A Final Message To The Abused

I hope that reading this book has been useful in helping you solve problems in your relationships. If you are in an abusive relationship, I truly empathize with your situation. I have finally felt your pain. I know the pain is inflicted unjustly, and that abusive words cut into you like daggers, destroying your self-esteem and causing you to feel hopeless. If you are currently in an abusive situation, there are only three choices you can make:

– First, you can continue in the abuse. If you do, the cycle will continue, the abuse will become more and more painful, and the time between each abusive episode will get shorter and shorter.

– Second, you can leave the relationship, if you like, and if you feel you must, I encourage you to make a list of positive and negative things to help you make the wisest possible decision. Ask yourself, "Can this relationship be saved?"

– If so, you have a third choice. You can confront your abusive partner and insist that he get counseling. A separation may be necessary to help insure that he stays in counseling and to help you heal. Most ERMs need to be compelled into counseling before they will seek help.

– There is no fourth choice. The abuse always continues without proper counseling.

The Best Is Yet To Come

Your journey through recovery will be the most difficult, yet rewarding, experience you will ever encounter. Allow yourself to pass through the frustration, grief, and confusion by removing the numbing layers of anger and addiction, stored childhood pain, and incorrect core beliefs. This process will allow you to feel acceptance and love for yourself and others. You especially will be more tolerant and sympathetic toward the behavior of others. You will understand why people behave the way they do.

It can truly be the most rewarding of life's experiences for those who are willing to face their abusiveness. Those rewards include loving relationships with others, inner peace with yourself and your Higher Power, and success and achievement in work and play.

Robert Robertson

APPENDIX

Anger Journals are a great way to analyze your abusive behavior. Information is power. I gained insight into my abusive behavior and discovered the five situations and negative self-talk that were my biggest problem. Make copies of the following pages and fill them out after each incident.

ANGER JOURNAL

Date/Time _____ Intensity _____

Situation (describe in detail) _____

_____

Negative self-talk (exact words) _____

_____

Drugs/alcohol (y/n) _____ Physical signs of my anger:

(tension/blood pressure/cold hands/etc.) _____

What did I do? _____ Stuff feelings (y/n) _____

Take a time out (y/n) _____ Escalate (y/n) _____

Direct/Assertive (y/n) _____ Abusive (y/n) _____

Type of abuse inflicted:
(Emotional/Physical/Sexual) _____

What would have worked better? What will I do next time? ___

_____

Have I: (Answer yes or no)
Been good to myself? _____

Been doing physical exercise? _____

Been avoiding drugs and alcohol? _____

Been taking practice time-outs? _____

Been attending group meetings? _____

Been reading self-help books? _____

Been monitoring my self-talk? _____

What will my new self-talk be? _____

_____

ANGER JOURNAL

Date/Time _____ Intensity _____

Situation (describe in detail) _____

_____

Negative self-talk (exact words) _____

_____

Drugs/alcohol (y/n) _____ Physical signs of my anger:

(tension/blood pressure/cold hands/etc.) _____

What did I do? _____ Stuff feelings (y/n) _____

Take a time out (y/n) _____ Escalate (y/n) _____

Direct/Assertive (y/n) _____ Abusive (y/n) _____

Type of abuse inflicted:

(Emotional/Physical/Sexual) _____

What would have worked better? What will I do next time? ___

_____

Have I: (Answer yes or no)

Been good to myself? _____

Been doing physical exercise? _____

Been avoiding drugs and alcohol? _____

Been taking practice time-outs? _____

Been attending group meetings? _____

Been reading self-help books? _____

Been monitoring my self-talk? _____

What will my new self-talk be? _____

_____

Robert Robertson

ORDER FORM

If you wish additional copies of *Confessions of An Abusive Husband*, please fill out and mail this form:

Name _____

Address _____

City _____ State _____ Zip _____

1 copy	$10.95 *plus* $2.50 postage/handling
2-5 copies	$10.00 each *plus* $3.00 postage/handling per order
6 or more copies	$9.00 each *no charge* for postage/handling

Make check or money order payable to:

Heritage Park Publishing Company
P.O. Box 126
Lake Oswego, OR 97034

Robert Robertson